NEW ROAD & TRANSPORT
PLANNING OF ENTIRE
INDIA

NEW ROAD & TRANSPORT PLANNING OF ENTIRE
INDIA

UNDER THE THEME
HOW TO REVIVE INDIA?

SANJAY PARDESHI

PARTRIDGE

A Penguin Random House Company

To order additional copies of this book, contact
Partridge India
000 800 10062 62
orders.india@partridgepublishing.com
www.partridgepublishing.com/india

! INSPIRATION !
RAJIV DIXIT

'**Rajivbhai**', a brilliant hardcore patriotic genius was working 20/22 years constantly for the nation.

The two things he focused were '**Swadeshi**' & '**How to revive India . . . ?**'

He believes that revival of India can be made through Swadeshi & formation of **Basic Revolutionary Plan Department (BRP).**

Though India has a number of problems, he wishes to reform basic six systems under **Basic Revolutionary Plan Department (BRP).** These six systems are

1. Economic revolution
2. Agriculture
3. Education system
4. Health & fitness system
5. Judicial system
6. Government & administration system.

He had given more than 10000 speeches on various subjects & travelled across the country day & night. His fluent speeches inspired millions of people to work for the nation.

We talk about the state of our nation anytime, anywhere! We get frustrated with all the political parties & decide they should be relieved from the responsibility of steering the nation . . . . or get nervous and lament 'Oh what's the use of our heated debating?! It'll remain the same whoever gets elected . . . . , and continue with our daily life.

WHY?

Is voting the only duty we have towards our nation? Have we become so selfish that we are in no way concerned with our country? Or are we really the losers . . . ?

If it is not so, please read on and join us! Now is the time to revive India with a renewed passion!

HOW?

When you go for revolutionary ideas/work
at first people just laugh
then they say "yeh to pagal hai!"
then they challenge you
then they ignore you
then they became jealous
& then they admire you!
Why . . . ?
Because, by then, you are already successful!

! VISION !

Road system in a country must be like veins in the body, that nourish public transportation, delivering complete safety and ensure smooth flow.

! THANKS !

To all my relatives who instilled confidence in me since childhood . . . !

To Mr. Mangesh Kadu & Mr. Atul Sathe for their beautiful DTP work and sketches . . . !

To Mr. Parag Patharkar, Ravi Sant & Gauri Deshpande for neat translation . . . !

To my wife "Vaijayanti" & daughter "Rutvika" for their thought-sharing . . . !

AND

To every patriotic person committed to the nation . . . !

SANJAY PARDESHI CONCEPT

Name: Sanjay Harising Pardeshi
Address: Country—India, State—Maharashtra,
                District—Pune, Pin Code—411004,
                Area—8, Yogeshwari apartment,
                above IDBI bank, Erandwane,
                Mehendale garage road.
Phone no.:   +91-020-22923998 / +91-020-25450070
E - mail: sanjay@spc1.org
Website: www.newroadtransport.com

CONTENT

How to Revive India?

There are many drawbacks and insecurities in today's Indian road and transportation system due to which the percentage of road accidents is on the rise. These are mostly affecting two-wheeler travelers who lose their lives on Indian roads every day. This will continue to happen in future if corrective measures are not taken. In the survey conducted by the **'National Criminal Registration Board (NCRB)'**, it was found that **26.5%** two-wheeler travelers get killed every year in India. Similar results were also published by the **'World Health Organization' (WHO).** According to the survey, India ranks first in fatal accidents. The most alarming fact noticed was that 66% of the people who lost their lives in Indian road accidents were in the age group of 18 to 50. **Isn't this a dreadful situation?**

(Reference: "Sakal Newspaper" dtd. 02.11.2011)

Therefore, to reduce these accidents, we have provided a separate lane for two-wheelers in our plan. Two-wheelers will travel through separate lanes in every part of India, i.e. villages, cities, highways, expressways. etc. **Does this type of system exist in the world?** Hence India needs to standardize its road and transport system. In this book, we present our **'New Transport System = Security of Travelers'**. Our system comprises separate lanes for two-wheelers, four-wheelers, trucks, buses, cycles, etc. There will also be standardization of buses and bus-stops to ensure safe transportation, so that passengers can travel without worry and return home safely.

Keeping the above things in mind, let us also understand a few other important points.

We all know that India is facing enormous problems in major areas in the form of corruption, huge economic rift in lifestyle of people, unemployment, unplanned development, poverty, suicides of farmers, and so on. Most of these problems are inter-related.

These issues divide our country in two parts. **20% of people are 'INDIAN', and 80% of people are from 'BHARAT'.**

In India, there are 50 to 60crore people earning less than Rs. 50 per day. Most of these are struggling even to satisfy their basic needs such as food, shelter, water, electricity, education, health, justice, roads, and importantly, value-added agricultural products. We have been working on all these issues for past 10/12 years. **Our main inspiration is Late Shri. Rajiv Dixit** (unfortunately, he is not with us anymore. He passed away at the age of 43 due to heart failure). Our concept starts with the question—**How To Revive India?**

A total change is necessary for a comfortable and pleasant lifestyle for Indian people. Since India is facing many problems, we have classified important problems in two distinct parts. We has arrived at a twelve point plan to tackle these problems. This program is titled as **Twelve Point Plan**.

Twelve Point Plan—T.P.P.

This action plan will decide the basic change needed along with a module for India's development for the next 25/30 years. As India does not have an ideal consolidated image in front of the people, different government offices work independently in their own manner. There is weak co-ordination between them since centralized co-ordination system for the consolidated development hasn't been strong enough. They do not have a combined ideal image of developed India. As a result, progress of India is unplanned and is not channelized properly. Hence, basic changes and development plans are essential and they must be considered collectively in a properly coordinated manner. We have made this pattern in the following ways:

A. Basic Revolutionary Plan (B.R.P.)—Six Main Problems
B. Infrastructure development Plan (I.D.P.)—Six Main Problems

A. Basic Revolutionary Plan (B.R.P.)

1. **ECONOMIC REVOLUTION:**—'Arthakranti' Action plan is ready in a complete form. Implementing this plan will result in a 'Tax free' and prosperous India.
   Main solutions of Arthakranti Foundation are
   (Reference: www.arthkranti.org):
   a. At present the taxpayers are paying 32 types of taxes to the government. Arthakranti proposes zero taxation throughout the nation (except the customs/import duty taxation). Today's taxation system will be terminated.

b. Only 2% bank transaction tax will be applicable to the payment receiver. This 2% tax will be distributed between Central Government (0.7%), State Government (0.6%), local governments (0.35%) and the concerned bank (0.35%).

c. The currency notes of Rs. 100/-, Rs. 500/- and Rs. 1000/- will be scrapped and will not be printed in future. Such large denominations are not used in developed countries.

d. Cash transactions above Rs. 2,000/- (Rs. 5000/-) will not be promoted.

e. All the black money deposited by Indians in different countries will be brought back and declared white money. The same shall apply for black money within India as well. **All these changes will be made at one stroke.—Proposal by Mr. Anil Bokil.**

Some other important points:

a. Our currency devaluated very fast after 1991. Our currency devaluated six-fold from 1948 to 1990. **(In 1948, 1 U.S. Dollar = Rs. 3 approx. whereas in 1990, it was 1 U.S. Dollar = Rs. 18 approx.)** After this period, our currency devaluated very fast **(1 U.S. Dollar = Rs. 50 approx.)** The reasons told were lack of foreign funds, recession, repayment of huge loans, etc. After this, the situations improved and our currency became strong up to **1 U.S. Dollar = Rs. 43 approx. in June-July 2011.** Suddenly, up to May 2012, our currency devaluated again **(1 U.S. Dollar = Rs. 56 approx.)** Why? Again, those in power told citizens about heavy recession in the world, huge loans taken by some developed countries, etc. At the same time in India, things were at par more or less. There were not many changes happening in India. Still only the Indian currency devaluated substantially. When India had recession and it took loans, its currency devaluated. However, when other countries took loans and went into recession, their currency didn't! Why was it that the only currency that devaluated in this period was the Indian currency? How did this happen? A major country had taken the largest loan in its history in June-July 2011, yet its currency became stronger and Indian currency devaluated. **Again such type of situation arises in August/September 2013 and Indian rupee devaluated up to Rs. 68 = 1 USD.** How could this happen again and again? Could none of our leaders (from any party) realize this? On the contrary, instead of prosperity, dearth has increased day by day in India. Why so? Is our entire economic and political systems are helpless? Do our economists, senior professionals and experts not realize these facts? And if they do, why they didn't provide a perfect solution? Everyone was only discussing! Fact is that devaluation of our national currency is the leading cause of our nation's condition and poverty. We have to make a proper revaluation of our currency. The value of our currency has to be improved. For instance, in countries like **Saudi Arabia** and **Qatar**, 1 U.S. Dollar equals 3.7 Riyal & 3.65 Riyal. This ratio has stayed as it is for many years. So, we must ask who is forcing the devaluation of Indian currency? At the same time, some countries have improved the value of their currencies overnight. This means we have to make our revaluation powerful in competition with other countries. **B.R.P.** department will study this in detail.

b. After implementation of Arthakranti, thousands of bank branches will have to be established due to limited cash transactions, say, up to Rs. 5,000/- This will generate high employment. If these banks are run from 8.00 AM to 8.00PM (in two shifts) all the transactions will be smooth.

c. To improve the economic stratum of a common man (workers, coolies, small farmers, drivers, etc.), the monthly salary of a person must be min. Rs. 15,000/-
This will be applicable in the entire nation, both in public and private sectors. Maximum salary should not be more than, say, 20-25 times than the minimum salary. This means that **the income and the currency rate should be kept steady** in such a way that small businessmen and poor farmers also should get Rs. 15,000/- per month. We will draw an action plan which would encompass the whole country's majority population (except some major positions) in one single largest group. Such type of salary structure is being followed by the **American President Barrak Obama** who has taken this step ahead. In America, the salary of the person at the lowest rank is around 2,000 U.S. Dollars per month and 20,000 dollar per month at the highest (except some major positions). Majority of people in America fall in this group. **Due to this method, the economic difference between the rich and the poor gets reduced**. 'B.R.P.' department will work on all these issues in detail.

2. **Agriculture:** If all farmers of India decided not to produce much agricultural products except their own needs, what will we eat? How shall we survive? We will have to purchase from other sources. But at what cost? We have to take this issue very seriously. If this happened suddenly, what will be the situation? On the other hand, farmers' suicides have not stopped, for which both, we and the government, are responsible. Farmers put their funds throughout the year, work hard and the government decides profits and selling rates of the produce. Is this possible in any other industry? Except for farmers, who will run this loss making business? If no one, then what are our responsibilities? No one ever thinks of it! **Now everyone shall and must think.** There has to be profit ability for the farmers. For balanced, profitable and good quality agriculture, a separate action plan will be implemented from ground level to top level. B.R.P. department will prepare this complete action plan and execute it properly.

3. **Education System:** A balanced, complete educational system with reasonable fees should be offered to the people. Free education for economically backward people should be made available, too. The Gurukul system that existed in India for thousands of years was replaced by the colonial government with a new 'convent' system, which still continues in India. The muted division of our people - 80% people from 'Bharat' and 20% people from 'India' - is a result of the major drawbacks in the 'convent' system adopted by us. We have to remove this disintegrated system and establish a new strong education system which will be available in all the major Indian languages. **(A special point here: Oxford university of England is following 'Gurukul' education system for the last 600 years,).** To make every student wise and a good citizen, a totally new curriculum will be prepared by education experts. Every student can avail the entire education in his/her mother tongue.

Such education will be available from 1stStd. to a Doctorate Degree, for all branches of knowledge. Students can choose alternative Hindi and English languages, too. The **Percentage Method** will be closed in future. Students can select any type of practical education of their choice. Educational experts and **B.R.P.** department will execute the new education system.

4. **Health and Fitness System**: Facilities in this action plan should be affordable to everyone, even to very poor people. **B.R.P.** department shall establish or launch a separate free health program for poor people, with the help of government officers/medical practitioners.

5. **Judicial System:** India's existing judicial system is deemed to be a very critical and slow system in the world. In the **business index** of World Bank for 183 countries, India's rank is 132nd, even lower than the **Gaza strip** nation. **This is a shocking truth**. Because of this faulty judicial system, even after so many scams/leaders/officers/servants pay nominal fee to the court and are release on bail. The same leaders then sit in parliament, too. The worst part is that they are welcomed in their community with processions as they are ". . . only suspects and not yet proven guilty". **What a strange judicial system!** Neither scammed money of these people gets seized nor are they punished heavily. **These people have now become our 'OWNERS'.** In this peculiar judicial system, neither terrorists like 'Kasab/Afzal Guru' are hanged immediately (they were hanged in 2013), nor are scam buildings like 'Adarsh' destroyed. This is because this judicial system was established by the British to ensure that Indian people would not get justice easily. Even today, the some Indian courts are enjoying yearly summer holidays for 25-30 days. The British implemented this tradition for their own convenience. No other governmental department has this facility. Thus, even after waiting for years and spending time, money and efforts, we are unable to get justice in time. This 150-year-old obsolete and slow-moving British judicial system has to be changed. We have to introduce a new judicial system which will be uncomplicated, transparent and fast through which people will get fair decisions in lesser time. **B.R.P.** department will have to work deeply on such judicial system with the help of respective experts.

6. **Government and Administration System:** Existing government system was formed mostly according to British laws and rules. This was primarily for ruling our country, encouraging slavery and exploitation. E.g. the British Queen offers some rooms in **'Buckingham Palace'** on rent for the sake of the nation. At the same time we are expending millions of rupees to maintain the prestige of our president **(Rashtrapati)**, a tradition totally unnecessary for a poor country like India. Today, the President of Turkistan lives in a small flat. He appealed to all politicians and ministers to do the same, and they agreed to it.

The Turkish President has thus reduced all unnecessary expenditures. Now for the last decade Turkistan is considered a developed country in Eurasia. **Even today, the President of Switzerland and many celebrities very commonly use railways and bicycles for journey.** In developed countries, government security departments manufacture various consumer goods, too, along with weapons and other security material. **This is called modernization.**

On the other hand, there are 34,575 different laws, rules and regulations in our system which were formed during the colonial rule. These laws, rules and methods are totally outdated, and are causing India enormous harm. This is one of the reasons why people in India are not getting the complete benefit of our country's development, though different governments have ruled us for the last 66 years.

It is our bad luck that even after 66 years of independence; we are still following such outdated methods and rules that encourage huge corruption. To change this situation, all of us need to be up-to-date and should try to save each rupee of our country. All such rules, methods and laws will be amended to suit today's conditions. E.g. After 75 years of age, no one shall be allowed to work in government and private sector. He/she can only provide consultancy without remuneration/fees. At present a really old person, aged 80-85 years, can get himself elected for the post of Prime Minister/Chief Minister/President/other post more than once. How can we proclaim India to be a nation of youth? Now such things shall be put to an end. Similarly, no one shall hold the same designation more than twice. If we want clean and fast development progressing on the right track, we have to make such type of fundamental changes in this 150-year-old, corrupt pattern of the government system. For this, a new action plan will be made. This is one of the hardest tasks to be carried out by **B.R.P. department.**

Expecting continuous discussions on these serious issues.

B. **Infrastructure Development Plan (I.D.P.)**

7. **Water System:** Making water available, its collection and distribution system. Our priority is to make clean drinking water available to all the **121 crore** people. Secondly, water should be made available for agriculture purposes. For this, activities like a River Linking program, building small dams/new lakes, canals, etc. need to be carried out. For this, appropriate action plans will also be made/implemented. I.D.P.

section will work with the administration and provide platform for experts and organizations working on respective issues. As a result, these activities will be understood and appreciated by people. This is one of the most important issues, and I.D.P. will work for a solution on priority.

8. **Electricity:** The system includes generation, collection and distribution of electricity. Action plan will be made for every type of electricity generation.
I.D.P. will work on thermal, hydro, solar, wind and nuclear electricity generation. It is necessary to create a detailed program by anticipating the demand and supply of electricity for the next 30 years. Organizations and experts having 20-25 years' relevant experience will be included in I.D.P. team.

9. **Drainage and Waste (Garbage) Handling System:** Instead of just discussing and criticizing the 'unclean India', let us have a proper action plan and details to convert open drainages into closed ones, arrangement of septic tanks, garbage disposal systems, making fertilizer, generation of electricity from the waste, etc. This action plan will be run by I.D.P. department under the indigenous **"National Hygiene Campaign". The Author is working on complete drainage/waste management system for entire India.**

10. **Residential Infrastructure:** It is necessary to fulfill basic needs of everyone at affordable cost. Proper living place or residence is the prime one. Main issue in this is the availability of developed land. However, please note, **all the efforts are worthless if population is not controlled.** Our land is approx 1/3rd that of the USA, whereas the population is approximately four times. This crucial segment will require stringent government control. Generally the prices of most goods and products increase every year by 10-15%. In some case, the prices remain unchanged or even get reduced. However, the prices of land in India have increased enormously, and will continue to do so every year. Why is it happening? Rates of lands are increasing by 100%, whereas our annual development rate is 10% max. It is a very serious matter and unless we control the increasing rates of a land, owning a house will remain just a dream for the common man. Even if we save more money in actual infrastructure, it is still less than the money we may spend in acquisition of land. **E.g.** In big cities like Delhi/Mumbai/Pune/Chennai/Kolkata, construction cost of an

average house is Rs. 1300/- to 1500/- sq. ft. In villages, it is around Rs. 1100/- sq. ft. Even if the government offers any tax-concession or the builder gives discount, the cost will be around Rs. 1000/- to 1300/- per sq. ft. in cities and Rs. 900/- to 1000/- per sq. ft in villages. It is possible to reduce cost by 10%. But what about prices of land? Due to the uncontrolled rise in the land prices, it has become a huge business for many to buy and sell land. Even the people who are working or want to work or can work in the interest of nation, all who want to contribute in social work are dealing in land because no other business can offer you such high returns in the shortest possible time. **Why is this going on?** Our condition will become pitiful after 50 years, if we continue to auction the land to each other.

Therefore government has to control the entire situation and must change the **Land Acquisition and other acts** as per today's conditions. It is imperative to think on various suggestions, action plans and solutions to address this matter. Some solutions are as follows:

a. Rates of agricultural land, vacant land, industrial plots, and houses/flats will be much more affordable if the rate of land and construction increases by 10% to 15% yearly and not more.

b. Rates of vacant land, agricultural land and construction cost will be decided by the government/administrative bodies from respective area. This system is in use today to some extent; however, it is very weak and ineffective. Percentage of black money in many such transactions is huge due to cash transactions. Creation of black money will be restricted if B.R.P. controls the prices **(Ref. Economic Revolution)** which will compel people to purchase and sell land/properties at predetermined rates by the government.

c. Registration of plots/buildings should be done only within a certain periphery. Registration will not be possible from other faraway places. Each individual can own maximum 2 plots and two constructed premises. The constructed premises should not be more than 5,000 sq. ft. and open plots not more than 20,000 sq. ft. Companies/organizations etc. can own larger premises as they need expansions. Farmers can own maximum 25 acre (1 acre = 40000 sq. ft. approx.) agricultural land individually. This rule will be for 400 km. After 400 km, the same person can own land, residence, agricultural land as per above. In this way government will be able to control/regulate property rates and quantity. If the government doesn't implement such type of ideas and rules from now, there will not be enough land available for **121(+) crore** people in coming years. Only rich people will own the lands/houses.

But it will be possible for a common man to own his shelter if above ideas/rules gets executed. I.D.P. section will work on this in detail. However our aim should be clear that each person should get minimum 100 sq. ft. place comfortably in his/her own house. Effectively, a family of 4/5 people should get a 400 to 500 sq. ft. house at a reasonable rate.

11. **New Road System for India:** it's the details are provided later in this publication.

12. **Transport System from Villages to Cities**: Details are provided later in this publication.

    Together, we all shall try to find a perfect and workable solution for all the above problems in the open forum called '**How to Revive India . . . ?**'

    '**How to Revive India . . . ?**': Our local/State and Central government have independent departments to work on the above mentioned issues. Unfortunately, people are not fully aware of these government systems. Also, people are not contributing their time, imagination and knowledge to study and understand these matters.

    Consequently, in most cases, the local population has different issues and needs, whereas the solutions offered by the government are irrelevant and far from the reality. This also leads to wastage of time and money for everyone. To avoid this, people should be made aware of all these government systems and methodology. **There should be consistency & synchronization from bottom to top along with BRP & I.D.P. dept, will be the soul of 'How to Revive India . . . ?'**

    Today's government officers/executives/experts/staff are unable to communicate with general public after a certain limit. They are unable to implement a firm solution for the progress of the country and the society. There is an urgent need of a '**Think-Tank**' having knowledge and foresight to fulfill this shortage. This think tank will present its ideas and action plans, **i.e. 'VISION PLANS'** to the government. All the developed countries have such think tanks which are a great way for achieving progress of the entire country. **This think tank will work transparently and independently for the nation only.**

Lack of innovation and unwillingness to implement perfect solutions are the biggest shortfalls in the present administration system. At the most, we do nothing more than discuss, write letters give suggestions or protest. If we get a facility such as **think tank of 'How to Revive India . . . ?',** where we can contribute from the **Concept level to Completion,** this will be a bigger step towards the development of India.

All the developed countries have made progress on their own strength and because of their own citizens. In Japan, people used to work 14 to 15 hours daily in the times of national crises. Developed countries never compromised on quality and gave the first priority to improvement and development. In such countries, all the political parties (whether it is the ruling party or the opposition) together think of the nation first. This is **REAL SWADESHI.** All Indians should develop our country in the same manner. Development and welfare of our nation should be our first priority. Political parties and individual gain should be set aside while focusing on the development of the nation. This is the only way people can unite and move forward. Developed countries have gone through the same process and we need to do the same as soon as possible with a difference. The re-creation of our nation in this manner will give us tremendous joy and happiness, which we are missing at present.

Let us start and participate in this journey of success and joy now!

Important Decisions

1. Obviously there will be innumerable discussions, difference of opinion, action plans, suggestions, changes, etc. However, the people and the government authorities will have faith in the **B.R.P.** and **I.D.P.** departments. The decisions taken by the people working in the above departments will be firm and final.

    There will be no interference from political, govt. or administrative authorities in these depts. However, there will be continuous interaction with each other.

2. The staff of these departments will draft Action Plans, and make estimates for complete planning. The Government/administrative authorities will have to execute the same. Without their proper cooperation and harmony, the entire process will be a futile exercise.

3. Along with the action plans, **B.R.P. and I.D.P** departments will take responsibility of consultation, supervision, execution and quality

control as well. These two departments will work through the 'Concept-to-Completion' stages and will take care of maintenance too.

4. Documentation required for these action plans, permissions, funds should be provided by the local corporations/Government/administrative departments in totality. This shall overcome the objections and difficulties to maintain work efficiency. They have to make sure the projects get executed on time.

5. A special power will be given to these departments in villages as well as in cities. Govt./admin. Departments should implement the same. They will also benefit fully since their employees are, ultimately, the 'people', too.

THE SUCCESS RATIO OF THESE DEPARTMENTS WILL DEPEND UPON THE GOVERNMENT ASSISTANCE.

We all will try to solve these problems with the local/state/central governments under the **B.R.P. and I.D.P** departments with revolutionary changes. **'How to Revive India . . . ?'** will be done under a twelve point plan. Here, we have made an action plan for **Roads and Transportation Systems** jointly. Following is the categorization of cities on the basis of their population:

1. **Mahanagar** : 40 lac* to 150 lac and above.
2. **Nagar** : 20 lac to 40 lac*[*1 lac(lakh) =0.1 million]*
3. **City** : 5 lac to 20 lac
4. **Village** : 1 lac to 5 lac
5. **Kheda** : 50,000 to 1 lac.
6. **Bastee** : upto 50,000

There will be small roads in Kheda, villages and in hilly areas while the biggest roads will be in Mahanagar. The necessary concept/key plans/sketches are enclosed herewith **(page no. 54 to 190)**. Two major parts of the same are:—

1. Standardization of the road features (incl. width) and transportation rules are shown on the **page no. 54 to 147**. These will be applicable in cities/Nagar.

2. For intercity and interstate roads (i.e. for roads outside city limits) the standardization is shown on the **page no. 149 to 177**. If we all can understand the new road system and convert the existing roads accordingly, 90% Indian roads will automatically be smooth and safe.

The structure and standardization of new roads has been designed such that existing roads can be converted, rapidly and economically, into the nearest standard. In short, one state-way, two highways and one expressway will make 90% transportation smoother. There will be different systems for villages and cities, and more secure and wider expressways around Mahanagar.

What type of action plans are being applied for the security of traffic and road system at present?

a. We are constructing over-bridges/flyovers and subways.

b. Instead of tar roads, we are building concrete roads which are more expensive. In future, we will construct strong tar roads instead of concrete roads. They cost much less and are easy on maintenance. Around the world, there are not too many concrete roads since they are very expensive to build and maintain. **We are breaking the existing tar roads and are building concrete roads which is a waste of our national wealth.** On concrete roads, the friction with tires is more causing more noise and tire-bursting accidents. This is a major problem with our roads today where the main issue is being neglected. I.D.P. department will work on it in detail.

c. Government is going to launch new metros, monorails, skywalks, etc.

d. **Central B.R.T. (Bus Rapid Transit)** system is being implemented. There are right side doors in these buses due to which sitting capacity of these buses is reduced. Local govt. is going to implement this plan in many cities, but these are very costly, need sizeable changes, and take a long time. The government should re-think these plans. Even after the implementation of these plans, we will have to create the basic outline for roads and the traffic systems as per the given sketches. Considering this fact, we have to make the minimum changes in the existing Infrastructure system before starting the metros, B.R.T., monorails, etc. **Hence we can go for SPC edgewise BRT (Refer page no. 183 to 189)** we have taken some concrete decisions to execute the above plan as per given sketches and layout.

As we all know, India is a developing country; in next 25/30 years it will be a developed country for which we have to be accommodative in all these matters.

It is necessary for us to adopt positive attitude and work hard for our nation. So let us unite and make our village/city/basti a successful role model for India.

ACTION PLAN

A. Road Planning.

1. **Width of the Road**:—The most important thing in road planning is that all the roads should have the same width till the end. This rule is mandatory in all the developed countries. Some important benefit of this is as follows:
    a. Security—for everyone.
    b. Systematic and methodical transportation.
    c. Reduction in number of accidents.
    d. Less number of traffic jams leading to fuel saving and efficient services.
    e. Reduced air/noise pollution as less people will use horns. For this purpose, the **IDP** department will introduce a **'Road Width Team'.**

2. We will have to deal with all the difficulties successfully in order to confirm the width of roads. E.g. some roads suddenly become narrow at some points because of various types of obstructions. To avoid this situation, we will have to convince the people from the respective villages, village councilors, corporate officers, State Governments and administration to work together.
    a. The people affected due to road-widening will have to be rehabilitated immediately. If possible, we should provide space/building close to the affected point by providing special **F.S.I (Floor Space Index)/T.D.R. (Transferred Development Rights)** without bending the rules.
    b. Demolition of existing good roads and building concrete roads should be avoided as it is a complete waste of money.
    c. Only bus stops and traffic signs will be allowed to exist on every footpath. Everything else will be removed. E.g. advertising posters/hoardings/display stands which are placed outside the shops, etc. Electric and telephone poles will be placed at the end of the footpath width. Similarly we have to shift roadside

hawkers, barrows, etc., to appropriate designated places by ensuring that these people do not lose their daily earnings.

Then what about these people? Where will they go? They will be introduced in **'CHOTA PARIWAR'.**

3. **What is 'CHOTA PARIWAR'?:** Even though there are number of shopping malls and stores, many people still run roadside businesses. This is an integral part of India. Their daily wages should not be affected as we strive to introduce better roads. **"Comfort and happiness of poorest man" believes in Gandhiji's 'Antyoday'.** I.D.P. will establish a **'Chota Pariwar'** concept every 1.5/2.0 km. for these people. People from the respective villages, state government and Municipal Corporation all together will establish such **'Chota Pariwar** where all types of small businesses can be established and these people will continue earning their daily income. Format of these **'Chota Pariwar'** will be designed as per the respective areas. In big cities every 1.5/2kms, there will be a separate building of 10 to 12 floors for such families. In small cities buildings will be of 6 to 7 floors and in the villages buildings will have 2 to 3 floors.

Detailing of this will be done by a team of **'Chota Pariwar'.** This team will establish such small families and will always keep working for this section to run this scheme properly and successfully.

4. Parking on some select roads will be banned to keep the uniformity in transportation and traffic control. To get over the parking problem, the local government/administration will have to build parking areas after every 1.5/2.0 kms. Any private company prepared to build a parking slot will be offered concession. Stay order or fortifications will not be considered. Parking area is an important point. To work on it, a separate **'Parking Team'** will be constituted. The concept will also be applicable to **'Chota Pariwar Team.'**

5. While forming or establishing section such as **'Chota Pariwar'** and **'parking areas'** there are possibilities of many controversies, disagreements, arguments, etc. The same problem can occur with the 'Road Width Team', too. To work on such problems, **I.D.P. Quick Court** will be introduced by the I.D.P. department, which will give correct decisions within 8-9 weeks and keeping in focus the larger public interest. However, these courts will direct the concerned authorities to carry out the rehabilitation and valuation in a fast and perfect manner.

6. **Another important aspect:** All the footpaths and roads should be clean and leveled as per the sketches and classifications. If they are not so, the government/administration should work on it immediately. All the gutters should be closed by strong covers (lids)/top caps whether on road or footpath and should be leveled. There should not be any potholes and uneven surfaces. If such things are noticed anywhere on the roads/footpath, they should be repaired immediately (level should be maintained while repairing) otherwise the traffic will be disturbed like today's transportation. For all of these works 'Road Level Team' will be formed.

7. If we can unite parking area and Chota Pariwar after every 1.5/2 km, it will be very convenient. A lot of time and money will be saved and the security will also increase with that. For all these, we will have to work very fast as explained below:

    a. **'Chota Pariwar team'** has to be formed by giving it a special responsibility.

    b. **'Parking Area Team'** will implement the parking sketch on roads and selected areas.

    c. **'Road Width Team'** will be most important and will carry a large responsibility. This team will keep all the details of the town/city/village together and will work on it independently.

    d. **'I.D.P.' Quick Court:** Established to deal with all the possible problems related to the above, and would be responsible for taking the final decisions.
        These courts will have special responsibilities to save time, and after the decisions are taken by these courts, there will be no further appeals.

    e. **'Road Level Team':** This team will make sure that each road and footpath will be leveled. The job profile of this team will be to check for potholes, to make sure that there are no mud patches left, the whole road will have tar on it with the entire width tarred up to the footpath. Similarly, all the nearby places will be tarred from footpaths (i.e. up to the houses, shops and nearby compounds). The same rule will apply for national highways/state highways, etc. **All roads will have drainage system at their ends to drain the rain water.**

8. **'Number of Five Teams':** According to the classification of the population there will be one team for every 1 lac of population, from

each department. According to this rule there can be 150 teams for big cities with 150 lac population. For villages and outskirts of the cities, each team can cover 50/70 km area having 1 lac population. The area will be designated to each team. Depending upon the local requirements, I.D.P. department will decide the number of members and the scope of work of these teams.

9. There are water lines, drainage lines, electrical and telecommunication cables under the roads. If possible, all these systems should be under footpaths and all the manholes on the footpath/roads should be leveled properly so that it will be easy to maintain and there will be no traffic jams. Wherever this system will not be possible, these systems will be placed under the roads or along the road ends. **All overhead cables will be 6.1m high from the road to ensure smooth transportation of heavy luggage.**

10. We will have to make sure that there will be no sharp turns in places like 'T' junctions, internal roads, society roads, service roads, small/long roads and multiple road junctions. It is very important that all the corners be circular/spherical. Footpath corners will also have circular/spherical shapes. For typical curve details, **please refer page no. 105.**

11. It is very important to put tar on complete width of the roads up to the footpath. In India, on both sides of roads, there is loose soil without any tar on it. This result in mud and slush during rains which spreads on to the roads. It is one of the major hazards of today's roads. These cause accidents and danger for the pedestrians and drivers. Hence, it is crucial to put tar on the complete width of the road so that this fault of today's road system can be removed. There will also be full width tar roads, tar places where the roads are small or where there are no footpaths and where there are fences, houses and shops along the road. There will be no mud along the roads in the villages, cities and towns. Consequently, there will be no dust on roads in villages, cities, towns, etc. (All the developed countries like America or Dubai have similar systems).

All gaps between the footpaths/roads and the compound walls, houses, shops, etc., should be tarred for the benefit of all. It will be more beneficial if local government and small businesses carry out this work. The people who don't follow this rule will have to pay fine, and strict action will be taken against them. This will be applicable even for the highways/state-ways and other roads outside the cities/villages.

12. **Signal System:** Signal system will be compulsory in every city, villages—at maximum T-Junctions, crossroads, hospitals, schools, market and wherever needed. There will be a facility of a white light in every signal for pedestrians crossing the roads and will be synchronized with red/green light. One can traverse approx 2' (0.6m) distance in 1 sec. Considering this calculation and width of road, timings of the white signal will be decided so that crossing the road will be comfortable and safe **(refer page no. 109 to 112).** Synchronization of traffic signals and signals for pedestrians will be compulsory all over the India. Synchronization of back-to-back signals is also necessary. Signals will be on 24x7, i.e. 365 days, wherever needed even on highways and expressways. It is an important point to consider while planning the transportation and traffic system. It is our priority to implement synchronized signal system everywhere in 7 to 10 years. Also we have to publicize road details, traffic rules in cities, villages, on highways, expressways with traffic signs.

13. **Zebra Crossing/Parking/Lanes:** Three important points to improve the existing transportation system and to streamline the traffic system.
   a. Width of every road will be constant all over India. E.g. If we decide that the width of the road will be 40' (12.19m) after the survey, then same width should be maintained throughout the nation. In case of decreasing width (which anyway, is not supposed to happen after survey), we must remove obstacles in the way to increase the width. If roads are uneven in width, maintain the minimum width and increase width of footpaths or cycle tracks.
   b. All roads will have traffic signs/markings of lanes and parking lane markings wherever applicable. This will be compulsory once the survey/classification and standardization of that road is completed. This will be applicable to service road/road inside housing complexes, village roads or expressway.
   c. **Zebra Crossing:** In villages or cities, there will be zebra crossings of height 8" (0.20m) instead of speed breakers. Width of this zebra crossing will be designed from 3' (0.91m) to 30' (9.14m) as per the average number of people crossing. The same system will

be programmed on state-ways/highways and other roads. **There will be no speed breakers on any road in the country.**

Zebra crossing of width 3' (0.91m) to 30' (9.14m) and 8" (0.2m) height will be placed near bus stops (behind the bus) from where road is to be crossed **(Refer page no. 123 to 127).** Each strip of zebra crossing will be 1'6" (0.45m) wide and length will be from 3' (0.91m) to 30' (9.14m). The distance between two zebra crossing strips will be 1'6" (0.45m) only. This will be standardized throughout the nation. There will be 1 to 1.3 km distance between bus stops inside cities. Hence, there will be another zebra crossing in between the bus stops at a distance of 0.5m to 0.6m. Apart from the above, zebra crossing will be marked at hospitals, schools, markets, colleges, railway/bus stands and wherever necessary. Zebra crossing will not be 8" (0.2m) high where three/four/five roads join together since there will be a signal system. Otherwise all zebra crossings will be of 8" (0.2m) height throughout the nation. **No road in the country will be without zebra crossing.** Similarly, there will not be **a single road in the country without lane markings.** All lane markings/parking markings/zebra crossing have been shown on **page no. 54 to 172.** Automatic cameras will be fitted at some points due to which people will follow self discipline and will not cross the road anywhere except zebra crossings.

14. 15' (4.57m) wide road is necessary considering next 25/30 years. Actually, this is a very small width, but today also there are several roads of this width in cities/villages. Hence, we have kept the minimum width as 15' (4.57m) Smaller roads can be widened up to 15' (4.57m) Considering the above facts, outer city roads are standardized to be minimum 12' (3.65m) wide for one-way movement, and 24' (7.32m) wide for two-way traffic.

15. If possible, roads should be kept up to 25' (7.62m) wide for one-way in cities. This decision can be taken depending upon the local traffic conditions and situations. Start alternate one-way system for roads more than 25' (7.62m) wide where crowd/traffic is very high. **E.g.** In New York (USA), 50/60 storied high-rise buildings are also constructed around 80'/100' (24.4m/30.5m) wide roads. Still the traffic flows smoothly because of a fixed width of the roads, lane systems, no parking on roads, leveled road and one-way traffic. In the

same manner, we can regulate/control the traffic on narrow crowded roads.

16. **Footpath**: It is very important to see whether footpaths have a minimum width of 3' (0.91m) to 12' (3.65m) (according to the place available). **Roads without footpaths will not be allowed in any city or village.** Footpaths can be made wider according to the width of the road available. Footpaths will not be allowed out of the city/village in the places such as expressways and highways. But emergency lane will be made available on expressways.

    Remaining all the roads (like society roads, business complex and service roads etc.) will have footpaths. Check the availability of the area and make the footpaths according to that. The width of the road and footpath will be according to the given design standardization. We can increase the availability of space for footpath from the width of 3' (0.91m) to that of 30' (9.14m), depending upon the need and rush. **To decide the width of the footpath, firstly, it is necessary to carry out the survey.** Suppose the road is 55' (15.36m)/60' (18.29m) or 70' (21.34m) wide, but the width of the footpath has to be wider than the standard width given, then declare that road as 50' (15.24m) wide standard road, and the footpath will be made wider. Similarly, along with footpath, people need crossover bridges to cross the roads. For this, Crossover Bridges are necessary along with the staircases. **If possible, it is very important to have escalators instead of lifts** for these crossover bridges since lifts can carry limited number of people. Escalators are a better way for carrying more people. This system should be made available in places like bus station, railway stations, hospitals, etc.

17. Refer the sketches from **page no. 54 to 177.** Except for the width of the main road, it will also include all the other features such as service roads, over-bridges, footpaths, subways, space for U-turns, etc. This will be very important for highways and expressways. However, it will be very difficult to maintain these systems in cities. Hence, after the standardization of main roads, the other service roads should be built as per the availability of land and as per the standardization.

18. **Dividers:** The dividers of the internal city/village roads will be made from ø 3" NB 'B' class (75mm) pipes and will be 3'4" (1m) high **(please refer page no. 146).** If more road-width is available than necessary, make the dividers wider with greenery on it. Please note that

the above **standard pipe dividers** should be in the center of these wider green dividers. All the dividers on highways/state-ways/expressways will be as shown on **page no. 147.** Small trees or bushes will be planned in these 12' (3.65m) and 10' (3.04m) wide dividers and the greenery will be maintained. All these dividers should start from 4" higher than road level so they will be safe and have less possibility of damage. If an accident occurs, the vehicle will go directly in those 12' (3.65m) and 10' (3.04m) wide divider lanes and get stuck there.

19. **Bridges/Crossover Bridges/Flyovers/Subways:** The height of all the crossover bridges/flyovers in the country will be 20' (6.1m) from the road/ground. The clearance between two bridges of the 'Multi-tier Bridge System' will be 20' (6.1m). **The width of all the bridges in the country shall be as per the standardization (Refer page no. 149 to 154)**
However for subways, there will be two types of standards— **(A)** 10' (3.04m) and **(B)** 20' (6.1m) clear height **(refer page no. 149 to 154 and page no. 173 to 177).** If there is a need of footpath/side margin on the bridges, then width of the bridges will have to be increased accordingly.
Generally, sufficient places are not available in the cities for crossing the roads. Hence, single-storied/double-storied/triple-storied crossover bridges can be constructed as per page **no. 96 to 105.** On the other hand there are places available out of the city for crossing the roads. Hence, single-storied crossover bridges can be constructed as per **page no. 167 to 177.** All existing bridges/crossover bridges/subways may remain as they are (if possible try to convert the same to the nearest standardization). However, all new bridges/subways can be constructed as per the enclosed new standard.

20. **Important guide lines for the roads out of the villages/cities:**
    a. Both sides of highways/expressways should be 250 feet (76.22m) free from the middle of the road. It means 500' (152.44m) width is necessary in between the constructions of both sides of the road. Similarly, both sides of state-way should be 200' (61m) distant from the middle of the road. It means 400' (121.95m) width is necessary in between the construction of both sides of the road. Similarly both sides of all other roads should be 150' (45.73m) distant from the middle of the road. It means 300' (91.46m) width is necessary in between the constructions of both sides of

road. **This may be the need of the future since there may be expressways as per the I.D.P department's planning.** If this free width is not available on both sides of the road at present, we have to convince & educate the people gradually about the same, and put necessary hoardings on those roads at an interval.

b. There will be boards indicating speed limit in the city/out of the city wherever necessary. These boards will be at an interval of 20 to 25 kms. All vehicles will maintain the standard speed limit **(±10)**, otherwise photographs will be drawn through automatic cameras, and driver will have to pay heavy fine. A heavy fine will be charged for breaking the lane discipline & other rules also.

c. Standardization of internal and outer roads of Basti/Village/City/Nagar/Mahanagar has been shown in the sketches. This standardization (such as width of the road, lane system, parking system, zebra crossing, bus stop, style of traffic, etc.) will remain same for entire India. **We will try to convert the existing roads to match the nearest standardization.** E.g. If the road width is 17' (5.19m), increase it to 20' (6.1m) width or 15' (4.57m) width standard road.

If road width is 45' (13.72m), reduce it to 40' (12.19m) or 50' (15.24m) wide standard road. The same rule will be applied for state-ways and highways. If the highway width is now 80' (24.39m), decrease it to make it 70' (21.34m) wide or widen it to make it 90' (27.43m) broad. If road width is 65' (19.82m), change it to a 60' (18.29m) width state-way, or 70' (21.34m) wide highway.

B. Public Transportation System: The main divisions are as below:

a. Railway system: Long/short distance trains, locals trains, metros, monorails, goods trains.

b. Luggage vehicles from light commercial vehicles to trailers.

c. City Bus service (In village/city).

d. Intercity and interstate bus transport service.

e. Private transport such as auto rickshaw (a three wheeler), small taxi, big taxi and rural (share) taxi.

21. **Railway System:** Existing trains can be faster by 10% to 15% using existing infrastructure itself. E.g.—

All passenger trains will run at an average speed of 40 kms/hr.

All mail trains will run at an average speed of 60 kms/hr.

All express trains will run at an average speed of 70kms/hr.

All Shatabdi/Sampark Kranti trains will run at an average speed of 80kms/hr.

All Rajdhani/Duranto express will run at an average speed of 100kms/hr.

I.e. Passenger trains will take 25 hrs. to travel 1000 kms., while Rajdhani/Duranto express will take 10 hrs. for the same. All other trains will take time in between these. If we can manage to increase average speed of all trains by 10% to 15%, yearly turnover of Indian Railways will increase reasonably. At such times, new bogies and engines will be required. For this, the government can increase its bogie production capacity and subcontract manufacturing of additional bogies/engines to any established, capable indigenous industry-house, for instance the **TATA Group**. At present, the total management of railways is under government, resulting in slow pace of work and slow speed of the trains, too! However, if additional bogies/engines could be manufactured by such a group, **it will be truly 'SWADESHI'. 'SWADESHI' is to do the things in the interest of nation as per the national requirements by joining hands together.** Since we are 121 crore people we have to follow **Chinese** railway system and not **'European'** one. We do not require very fast trains like Europe. We can follow Chinese railway system with maximum number of comfortable trains ferrying more passengers at a reasonable speed. In today's scenario, the number of trains is less. We must try to increase the average speed of all express trains around 70 kms/hr (In China, it is around 85kms/hr). This gives following benefits:

1. Passengers will save their valuable time. They may prefer trains over airplanes.

2. Turnover of railways will increase. If speed of goods trains also increases by 10% to 15%, Indian Railways will definitely earn more.

3. Since we will introduce more trains/bogies, the problem of 'No Reservation available' will get minimized and more passengers would be able to travel.

4. Government department will manufacture more new bogies/engines and can get the same manufactured from private sector as well.

5. These can be accommodated in existing infrastructure with certain modifications. Even today, Express/Rajdhani trains are running between 90 and 130 kms/hr. Here we are suggesting increasing only the average speed.

6. Today, there are huge demands for the Garibrath/Rajdhani/ Duranto type of trains out of which the railways get more money. Similar is the case for AC bogies. Increasing AC bogies results into lesser number of 2nd class bogies. **However, these problems can be solved by increasing number of trains itself which is a 'must'.** The government officers, people, railway experts can study in detail, and try to achieve 10% to 15% more average speed. Thus, we can design the first **'Adarsh Railway'** around which we can build other things.

   Adarsh Railway: This refers to any clean express train which can travel at an average speed of 70 kms/hr and cover 1000 kms in 14 to 14½ hrs. Adarsh railway pattern could be as follows:

   1. Bogie for Luggage/others   = 1 No.
   2. Bogie For ladies/Handicapped   = 1 No.
   3. A.C. first class Bogie   = 1 No.
   4. A.C. two tier Bogies   = 2 Nos.
   5. A.C. three tier Bogies   = 4 Nos.
   6. Pantry (compulsory for all trains)   = 1 No.
   7. 2nd class bogies   = 8 to 10 Nos.
   8. General bogies   = 2 Nos.

                                 Total = 20 to 22 nos.

In today's scenario, **'GARIBRATH'** can be an **'Adarsh Railway'** with following modifications:

1. Presently, there are three berths on one side which are very congested. Hence, replace the same with two-berth design as a norm.
2. Bogie patterns will be as per the 'Adarsh Railway' in which 2nd class bogies will be the existing ones.
3. Remember, this train should run at an average speed of 70 kms/hr.

We may introduce some standardization under this **Adarsh system** such as:

a. Adarsh Railway
b. Adarsh Railway Station and S.P.C. Front Roads
c. Adarsh S.P.C. City Bus
d. Adarsh Intercity/Interstate Bus
e. Adarsh S.P.C. Bus Stand and Front Roads.
f. Adarsh S.P.C. City Roads, etc.

A BIG QUESTION: Are these mandatory changes possible in today's scenario?

Answer: The railway officers, employee, staff, IRCTC people took lots of efforts in the last 10/12 years resulting in a centralized computer reservation system, running of Duranto express etc. Even today, they are working on development of railway system. But one thing remains unchanged—there is no facility for other people, experts and passengers to contribute. Since it's a government organization, common man can't participate directly though his observations/suggestions may be valuable and useful. **E.g.**

Most railway stations and tracks are unclean with poor sanitation and lack of water. The basic reason behind this is the railway's faulty drainage system. There is no improvement in it. **The problem may be solved as follows:**

Each bogie have two + two = four toilets. Build all the four toilets 8" (0.2m) above the level of the train floor. People will have to climb one step (8" = 0.2m) to enter the toilets. However, due to this modification, an approximately 10½' (3.2m) long x 4' (1.21m) wide x 8" (0.2m) wide (including passage) collection tank will be available. **(Please refer page No. 48).** The waste and water for full day will be collected in this 0.68m³ (approx.680 liter) capacity tanks. Every train (including Duranto express) will stop daily between 8 A.M. to 10 A.M. in a station where suction system will be available. For this to work, we have to install suction system on that station beforehand.

This suction system will work opposite to the system of filling the water in the bogies. After the train stops, the main common suction pipe will be connected to each collection tank through hoses as shown. After suction system starts, all the waste and water from each collection tank will be sucked simultaneously through common suction pipe and will be collected at one end in bigger tank. (This waste and water can be use to make fertilizers and then for power generation). Remove all hose pipes; close the collection tank outlets before the train moves further.

For this system, we will further understand a few fundamentals:

1. All toilets will be installed with airplane-like air suction system to minimize usage of water. Usage of water should not be more than one liter per flush.
2. In India, water consumption in toilets is high. Hence, overflow is a must for each collection tank. The design of this overflow

should be in a manner that it will open automatically after filling of collection tank. Also, overflow design will be such that only water will drain and not waste.

3. Waste handling/suction systems will not be required at all the stations. They will be installed only at major stations where the trains stop between 8 and 10 AM. The new time table should be introduced accordingly.

4. A 680-liter collection tank will be sufficient for a day and for two toilets. However, other details, changes such as suction system design, new design of toilets, door, odorless toilets, application of non-return valves, etc., will have to be studied thoroughly.

5. Once the above system is planned and implemented, all railway stations and tracks will be clean like Hyderabad railway station. Railway officers/staff/experts, I.D.P. dept. and people will join hands and will come up with fool-proof solutions. The government and companies dealing in waste handling will come into force.

6. New train bogies can be manufactured with this type of new toilet design. However for existing train bogie, a separate collection tank of approximately 600 liter capacity with proper dimensions can be manufactured and fitted below the toilets.

22. Local Trains:

A. We read about people falling from the local train because of heavy rush. In today's scenario, the number of local trains is fair enough. The only problem is lack of discipline and management. **Traffic discipline is essential for such huge rush;** otherwise these types of accidents will happen time and again. Here are some solutions to resolve the problem:

1. All local trains will have separate doors for getting 'IN' and 'OUT'. Because of this **Unidirectional Traffic System (U.T.S),** people will stand in a queue on the markings **(refer sketches on page No. 49 to 51)**and will enter the train easily.

2. There will be queue markings on each platform. There will be 'IN' and 'OUT' markings on the doors.

3. People should be aware of this new system. Hence, display the new method on the platforms along with the announcement.

4. To start with, try this method for some period in some stations and then apply it in totality.

B. Constant improvements are required in local train systems as these are the **'LIFELINES'** of all major cities. In today's development scenario, difference between the local trains and metros should not be more except air-conditioning system. More or less, the structure of both the trains may be same except metro will be air-conditioned. In due course, all local trains will also be air-conditioned. Considering the above criteria, we have made an outline of a local train bogie. **(Refer page No. 50 and 51).** People can easily get 'IN' and 'OUT' in this new type of local train and metro.

These two types of trains can be as follows (depending upon the local needs and the situation):—

1st bogie	: First class air-conditioned	- For gents	- 1.
2nd bogie	: First class air-conditioned	- For ladies	- 1.
3rd bogie	: First class air-conditioned	- For families	- 1.
4th bogie	: Second class	- For families	- 1.
5th bogie	: Second class	- For ladies	- 1
Others	: Second class	- For gents	-4 to 7

Total—9 to 12

Since we will be following the Unidirectional Traffic System (U.T.S) and will walk always from left side, these types of small but important standardizations are very essential so that traffic can be controlled automatically. Hence, blue arrow at left side will be painted on all railways over-bridges, footpaths, walkways, skywalks, markets, shopping malls, hospitals, bus stands and wherever they are easily visible to walking people. There will be displays on railway stations, in train bogies, in bus stands of this new system. **Education of people is a must for implementing any new method.** Similarly, display of entire route will be affixed in every bogie of each train which shows route stations, reaching time and distance. This facility will be available for long distance and other trains also. **This is the major flaw in existing railway system.** If it is displayed permanently in the bogies, it will be appreciated. However, it may not be possible because of changing of the bogies. Hence it should be affixed like a reservation chart. If possible this information can be displayed electronically in each bogie. This information should be announced at all stations and, if possible, in the bogies.

23. **Railway Station and S.P.C. Standards Front Roads:** Please **refer page no. 118 to 122.** In this, there are five types which include **Unidirectional Transport System (U.T.S.),** Symmetrical Parking System and Standard Roads. The main benefits for people are as follows:

1. In the above standardization, specific slots will be allotted for auto rickshaw/taxi/two-wheeler and car. Similarly, entrance and exit of stations will be situated only at specified places. Incoming and outgoing roads of a station will be constructed in a specific manner. Because of standardization, the main beneficiaries will be the passengers, who will follow the discipline.

2. There will be minimum traffic jams around the stations resulting in smooth and easy traffic which will gives comfort to everyone including driver.

3. The rush at the entrance/exit will be less due to the Unidirectional Traffic System & other standardization.

24. **Luggage Vehicles: The biggest drawback in the present public transportation system is the variety of vehicles travelling on our roads.** There is no system which has addressed this issue ever. A variety of buses, different types of trucks, trailers, LCVs, many 2 and 3 wheelers and taxies, and an occasional bullock cart are seen on today's roads. This leads to very slow moving, unorganized traffic without discipline. All the developed countries have standardized public transport carriers and goods transport vehicles (except private vehicles), resulting in a much regulated traffic. We have to remove this drawback by standardizing public transport combined with a standardized traffic system. Considering these points, we may standardize buses, trucks, LCVs, taxies, trailers, etc. as follows:

25. **Luggage Vehicle:** The main types will depend upon the maximum carrying capacity of LCVs and trucks. The trailers will have the maximum carrying capacity and length. Road carriers will be the second largest means of goods transportation after the trains. At present, this sector is neglected by the government and is quite unorganized. **Hence, we have to make some revolutionary changes in this sector.** India is a developing country and there will be sizeable growth in next 25/30 years. New big factories will be constructed for this development in which huge equipment will be required. These new equipment will be bigger in length, width and weight. These

types of equipment will play a major role in the development of India. Considering all these factors, we have categorized 12 types of luggage vehicles for standardization as follows:

Sr. No.	LCV	Maximum NettCarrying Capacity (without self weight of the vehicle)	Structure
1	Mini LCV	500 Kg.	Proper length and width
2	Small LCV	1000 Kg.	Proper length and width
3	LCV	2000 Kg.	Proper length and width
4	Large LCV	4000 Kg.	Proper length and width

We must keep in mind that three-wheelers are very unsafe for carrying luggage or passengers. The present three-wheelers also create air/sound pollution. Therefore, try to promote four- (or more) wheelers for transportation and travel.

Along with LCV, truck and trailer standardization may be as under:

Sr. No.	Truck	Maximum Nett Carrying Capacity (without self weight of the vehicle)	Structure
1	Mini Truck	7,000 Kg.	Proper length and width
2	Small Truck	10,000 Kg.	Proper length and width
3	Truck	15,000 Kg.	Proper length and width
4	Large Truck	20,000 Kg.	Proper length and width

Sr. No.	Trailer	Maximum Nett Carrying Capacity (without self weight of the vehicle)	Structure
1	Mini Trailer	30,000 Kg.	Proper structure and length - 20' (6.1Mtrs.)
2	Small Trailer	30,000 Kg.	Proper structure and length - 40' (12.19Mtrs.)
3	Trailer	30,000 Kg.	Proper structure and length - 60' (18.29Mtrs.)
4	Large Trailer	30,000 Kg.	Proper structure and length - 80' (24.39Mtrs.)

The complete transportation of the country will be carried out through these 12 types of luggage carriers. The point should be noted that all vehicle manufacturers will maintain the same standard within these 12 varieties. Other measurements may change, but length and width should not differ from the specified measurements. All vehicle manufacturers and government officers will make these new standards along with measurements which will be the same throughout the country.

Extra: Special purpose multi axle trailers/road trains have higher capacity of carrying luggage. Consequently, such vehicles are made separately. The number of such vehicles is very less. So, we will not consider them for our standardization.

However, the standardization of this vehicle may be as under:

Multi Axle Trailer	For special luggage, i.e. very lengthy, wider and heavy.	Proper structure and max. length 100' (30.48m)

If required, the vehicle of more than 100' (30.48m) length may be manufactured by taking special permission.

An important point about luggage vehicles: The width of luggage vehicles will not exceed 9' (3.74m) and the length will not exceed 80' (24.39m). Similarly, maximum permissible measurement of laden luggage will be the same for entire India, and it will be maximum 11' (3.35m) width X 100' (30.48m) length X 16' (4.88m) height.

If the luggage has more height and length then it should be designed in pieces as far as possible.

Power steering and good suspensions are compulsory for all type of vehicles.

We will further see the same standardization for buses (Total Type 7) and taxies (Total Type 4). As a result, there will be max. 23 type of vehicles seen on Indian roads as under:—

Light Commercial Vehicles	– Total Type	= 4
Truck	– Total Type	= 4
Trailer	– Total Type	= 4
Bus	– Total Type	= 7
Taxi	– Total Type	= 4
Total Type		**= 23**

Other private vehicles like carts, tractors, vehicles used for farming can travel only within a limited area around the workplace. They will not travel on 60' (18.29m) state-ways/national highways/expressways and on congested city roads. They can travel within 50 km. around the workplace. People will not be allowed to use these vehicles as passenger carriers. For that purpose, the usual public transportation should be used. In this way, there will be maximum 23 types of public transportation vehicles on the roads. This standardization will reduce the variety of vehicles in India by 50%. Consequently, the traffic will get corrected to almost perfection.

City Buses: All city buses will run on 25' (7.62m) wide (or wider) city roads as per **page No. 58 to 82**.

Maximum roads, buses, bus stops and transport systems have been standardized below for the safety of passengers and ease of travelling. Due to this, traffic discipline will also increase. **Following are the standardized city buses:**

1	Big Double Decker	40' (12.19m)long, 9' (2.74m) wide	Seat capacity 86
2	Small Double Decker	30 ½' (9.90m)long, 8' (2.44m) wide	Seat capacity 64
3	Big Bus	40' (12.19m)long, 9' (2.74m) wide	Seat capacity 49
4	Bus	30 ½' (9.90m)long, 8' (2.44m) wide	Seat capacity 39
5	Small Bus	25' (7.62m)long, 8' (2.44m) wide	Seat capacity 31
6	Mini Bus	20' (6.1m)long, 8' (2.44m) wide	Seat capacity 23
7	Micro Bus	15' (4.57m)long, 8' (2.44m) wide	Seat capacity 15
8	Share Big Taxi	Fare determined by local authorities	Seat capacity 12
9	Share Small Taxi	Fare determined by local authorities	Seat capacity 8
10	Private Big Taxi	With electronic meter	Seat capacity 5
11	Private Small Taxi	With electronic meter	Seat capacity 5

Please note that the seat capacity of the taxies includes driver.

The buses/auto rickshaws/taxies/LCVs/trailers/trucks which are running at present will run in the same manner. However, all new buses will come with the new standardization. Kindly note that power steering and air suspension will be compulsory for all types of new buses. Manufacturing of AC buses will be encouraged. Seeing the Indian roads and traffic, Double Decker Buses will be safer and convenient than articulated buses. With some modifications (E.g. only one front left door) the above buses can be converted into inter-city/inter-state buses. Except for the bus length, some minor modifications can be made in the measurements and number of seats. **Length of the buses and the door positions will remain unchanged as per the standard since the bus stops will be designed accordingly.**

Due to standardization of the buses in the entire nation, the benefits will be:

a. Manufacturing cost of buses will be reduced and all manufacturers will manufacture more or less identical buses resulting in economic rationalization.

b. After sales costs will be reduced as the spare parts can be interchanged.

c. The standardized bus stops all over the country will ensure ease and safety for the passengers **(Refer page No. 136 to 145).**

A very serious incident: In Pune city, in January 2012, a bus driver drove a public transport bus in a wrong lane causing 9 deaths and injuring many. He was caught and upon further investigation, it was found out that he was not a psychotic but was a normal person. **Then what was the reason for such a shocking behavior?** It was revealed later on that he got terribly frustrated due to the daily workload of 12/13 hrs., insufficient salary, poor working environment, declining state of buses, unavailability of basic power steering resulting in body pain, crowded roads and undisciplined traffic, unavailability of proper bus stops, terrible road conditions, etc. All these had a combined effect on him, and eventually he lost his mental balance. This case is a vivid example why we need to address this issue as soon as possible and arrest further deterioration of our public transport system. Our people and their lives are too precious to be lost in such a manner.

We need to implement the following systems in India at the earliest:

1. Standard width of roads so that all buses can move only in the left lane.
2. Good quality buses with standard specifications along with proper place for buses to stop.
3. Standardization of bus stops.
4. Separate left lane for all buses on all roads.
5. All buses to be fitted with power steering and air suspension so that drivers feel comfortable while driving. Manufacture of A.C. buses as much as possible to deliver comfort to both, passengers and drivers.
6. Proper zebra crossings and signals wherever necessary.
7. Reasonable salary for drivers/conductors with a workload of 7/8 hours a day.
8. Good quality rest rooms and good quality subsidized food for the drivers/conductors, (It will be available in **S.P.C. Adarsh Bus Stand**).
9. Introduction of discipline in the traffic and overall transportation system.
10. Good quality houses at reasonable rates for the families of drivers/conductors.

Our safety is entirely in the driver's hand whether he is a bus or train driver. Hence it is our social responsibility that all above facilities are made available to each and every driver. I am sure there will be a day in the near future when all the drivers will avail these facilities. I have taken maximum care about the same in my '**New Road and Transport planning of Entire India**".

26. A public transportation vehicle (bus, auto rickshaw and taxi) will travel in one lane only. Consequently, only taxies and rickshaws can overtake the buses. All buses will travel 100% along the footpaths or the parking lanes (without overtaking any one). Only if required, a bus may overtake another bus. In case a bus is following an auto rickshaw/taxi, they should move towards the right (and not left) so that the bus can continue travelling in the same lane without overtaking any other vehicle. This facility will be available only for city buses. For all other vehicles, overtaking from the right side will be legal. (Overtaking from the left side will be prohibited). On some roads, two-wheelers will have three lanes including a parking lane.

On such roads, overtaking from the left side for two-wheelers will be permissible **(Refer page no. 70, 72, 74 and 76).** These new rules and regulations will be demonstrated and advertised through the media.

27. **Electric Buses:** The fixed lane pattern is important to run electric buses. All city bus lanes are 100% specified in my lane system. An electric bus cannot overtake another electric bus. An alternative is that electric buses can travel easily in the following two types of structures:
    1. All electric city buses will travel along the length of the footpath. **(refer page No. 137)**
    2. All electric city buses will travel along the parking marks on the roads (area where parking is allowed on roads). **(refer page No. 137)** Bus stops on these routes can be fitted in parking areas. However if we can turn the electric cables in a proper manner, then this problem can be solved. In that case, a slightly more space may be required around the bus stops.

The main benefits in running electric buses are:
a. Manufacturing cost of the buses will be reduced automatically.
b. Air and noise pollution will be nil.
c. Diesel will not be requiring at all, savings millions of rupees.
d. Bus driving will be very easy and comfortable for the drivers, and will substantially reduce their fatigue.
e. The life of buses will increase.

We will have to take following measures to put the above system in place:
1. More electricity should be generated. There is huge consumption of diesel for the buses, which entails very high costs for the nation. We can start new power generation plants in these costs.
2. New electric cable lines to be put in bus lanes along with new poles which can be raised at one end of the footpath as shown. This work can be completed in the same cost that would be incurred to implement the new B.R.T. system.
   One should consider the scenario over the next 25/30 years. How much diesel will we require? What will be the cost? Then we may agree that electric buses is one of the best alternatives to achieve comfort, safety and economy too.

28. **City Bus Stops:** Today there are many types of bus stops causing inconvenience to people. In many cases, these are unsafe as well. To

overcome this we have standardized **six types of city bus stops for seven types of buses.** This will result in reduction of manufacturing and maintenance cost of the bus stops. **(Refer page No. 138 to 145)**. Standardization of the bus stops and dividers throughout the nation will reduce the production cost substantially **(for dividers refer page no. 146,147).** Bus stops and dividers will be made from two types of materials **(1)** stainless steel (S.S.) **(2)** Mild steel (M.S.) with powder coating.

Unidirectional Traffic System (U.T.S):—The design and standardization of Buses and bus stops will be done in such way that people will walk in one direction with discipline without getting crammed. The bus stops will be placed on the footpaths only and the width of the footpath will be 8' (2.44m) and11' (3.35m) at the point where the bus stops will be located **(Refer page No. 138 to 145)**. Bus stops can be kept max. 11' (3.35m) inside the footpath for stopping the bus while keeping the roads totally free. As a result the buses can halt at the stops without obstructing the traffic flow. The outer-city bus stops can be kept at a distance of 1.5 to 2 km. depending upon the population. However all outer-city bus stops will be 11' (3.35m) inside the footpath **(Refer page no. 127)**. This will be mandatory throughout the country. There will be 8" (0.2m) height zebra crossing (behind the bus) on every bus stop **(Refer page no. 123 to 127)**. There will be taxi/auto rickshaw stand at each bus stop (behind the bus) as shown in **page no. 91 to 94.**

This standardization will also bring in discipline among the taxi/rickshaw drivers. Since people will realize that at every bus stop, there will be taxi/auto stands and zebra crossing, they will maintain discipline while crossing the roads. Any violation may result in heavy fine.

29. **Interstate/Intercity Bus System:** We have standardized 'City Buses' in such manner that with some modifications, these buses will be used as interstate/intercity buses. The modifications will be **(1)** one left side door in the front, **(2)** improved and more relaxing chairs for long journeys, **(3)** Air conditioning **(4)** Berth, etc. Mini/small buses can travel to villages and hilly areas while the big buses will run on expressways. Double decker buses will travel inside cities/crowded areas. Please note that power steering and air suspensions are compulsory for all types of buses and we will try to build maximum

A.C, buses. **The seating capacity and other dimensions of these buses may vary** since bus stop standardization is not required for these buses. It must be noted that the bus stand for all these buses may be designed on the excellent concept of the bus stands in Mysore city of Karnataka State. There will be same types of small bus stands for small cities/villages. In the present scenario, there are neither good quality buses available with the government nor do we have good quality bus stands. In future the state government authorities will have to buy good quality buses and build good quality bus stands to match the Mysore bus stand. They can allocate some space for private companies for their buses. The fare of these private buses will be 10-15% more than the government buses. The real beneficiaries will be people of India, who will get good government and private buses with quality service at clean and neat bus stands at all times. **This is our MOTTO.**

Considering the above points, we have designed S.P.C. BUS STAND and Front Roads (refer page no. 113 to 117)

30. **Intercity Standard S.P.C. Bus Stands and Front Roads:** This concept is based on a single/two-storied fully equipped bus stands. We can change the existing bus stands into new S.P.C. bus stands with certain modifications, or we can demolish the existing bus stands and build new S.P.C. single/two-storied bus stands with new types of front roads. These bus stands can be air conditioned. The funds required for these new bus stands can be generated by selling the second floor to private bus owners or renting it. However for completing all this, we will require the necessary permissions from the local/state government transport authorities. Again, the main beneficiaries will be the people, which is our chief objective. People can easily reach new bus stands through new types of front roads without traffic jams and they will have the option to use the government or the private buses at any time.

    If people can enjoy travelling by the public transport they will reduce the use of private cars which will reduce the air/noise pollution and the fuel consumption as well. **S.P.C. Bus Stands** will be a very effective means towards solving the current public transport issues.

31. **Three-wheeler/Taxi:** Three-wheeler vehicles are not as safe as the four-wheeler vehicles, and are generally uncomfortable for the passengers. Hence, all the three wheeler manufacturers should start

manufacturing small LCVs/small taxies. In the coming years, new roads will be built as per the standard, new standard buses/taxies will be manufactured and new standard bus stop will be built. As a result we'll experience very neat and clean transportation system on the roads. For these, we will opt for four types of taxies:

Private Small Taxi : Nano, Indica, Alto, etc. Seat capacity: 5

Private Big Taxi : Manza, Indigo, DZire, etc. Seat capacity: 5

Shared Small Taxi : TATA S. Zip/Magic, etc. Seat capacity: 8

Shared Big Taxi : TATA Winger, Force Cruiser, etc. Seat capacity: 12

Today, there is no proper bus/taxi system in our villages. Hence, we propose to start city buses (as per the standard) to connect two nearby villages. For small villages, kheda, basti, encourage micro/mini buses with the help of local authorities. Local authorities also encourage rural taxies; such as Tata Venture, Maruti Ecco, Mahindra Maximo, Tata Magic, etc. There will be sufficient number of vehicles on roads avoiding crowding in one vehicle, which is dangerous and inconvenient for everyone. People violating the rules will be fined suitably. However, in the rural transport system, there will be no meters to decide the fares but a rate card based on the distances which will be decided by the local authorities. These changes will be done in the next 4/5 years. In India, there will be fresh two tone colors for all taxies like:

City Small Taxi : **Silver + Blue with Electronic Meter**

City Big Taxi : **Silver + Green with Electronic Meter**

Shared Small Taxi : **Silver + Dark Brown**

Shared Big Taxi : **Silver + Orange**

The existing taxies in Kolkata/Mumbai, etc. will run with their existing yellow/black color. The new taxies will come in fresh colors mentioned above. It will be mandatory to have an electronic meter in all taxies/rickshaws which will display km and fare. This **Electronic Meter System** will be implemented in all the states simultaneously and any violations will attract heavy fines/imprisonment. Fare for a share taxi/auto in a city and outer city will be fixed by the local government authorities.

Buses, taxies, rickshaws will be operated on C.N.G./L.P.G./Battery in future leading to lesser pollution.

32. Parking: There will be 'PARELLEL PARKING' on the roads for all vehicles throughout India (including two-wheelers). Today, we park two-wheelers at right angle to the curb-length. Due to this while getting out, a two-wheeler which is approx. 7' (2.44m) long has to turn through a right angle before moving off. These movements are potentially dangerous for the moving traffic. Such unsafe parking system is not common in other countries. Similar situation is applicable for three/four-wheelers. To avoid the above unsafe parking system, there will be no right angle/inclined parking on the roads. **Right angle/inclined parking will be in parking areas only.** All vehicles will be parked parallel on the roads **as per page no. 91 to 94.** Similarly in all upcoming buildings (such as residential societies, malls, multiplex, hospitals etc.) new parking standards will be implemented. E.g. F.S.I. (Floor Space Index)/T.D.R. (Transferred Development Right).

33. (F.S.I. Floor Space Index)/(T.D.R. Transferred Development Rights):
E.g. In Pune, many new prestigious commercial buildings have been constructed. In one such huge building (having many offices, shops and restaurants), sufficient parking spaces are not available at peak hours, and people are compelled to park their vehicles around the building wherever the space is available. This leads to chaos and disturbance. The reasons are:

a. 9/10 stories high, this building is situated on anapprox. 60'/70' (18.29m/21.34m) wide city road.

b. Due to heavy traffic, parking is not allowed on the road.

c. As a matter of fact, the building complexes are quite well-designed. However, considering the actual space required for parking (even though there is a 2-level basement parking), additional space should have been provided. Why is this so? Was the unavailability of the correct FSI the reason? Or the lack of foresight about space requirement? Or was it because of *more* F.S.I./T.D.R.? Could nobody visualize these consequences unanimously **since I.D.P. dept is not available?** To avoid all this, I.D.P. department has to go in detail for all new plans with new standards. That means first I.D.P. dept. will understand about the new construction *in totality* as follows:

1. How many floors will be constructed?

2. How much tenement density is allowed? What is the requirement? If more F.S.I./T.D.R. has been sanctioned, does the traffic get affected?

3. How much parking area is required for working people/residents (including visitors)?

4. The main question will be—how much is the road width in front of the complex/new construction?

5. To what extent will traffic increase due to this new construction?

Some solutions on these issues:

1. Local government authorities have to think in totality before sanctioning any additional F.S.I./T.D.R. to a builder. As the I.D.P. department is not present today, local officers cannot issue the permissions taking into account the road width, traffic conditions, tenement density, F.S.I., drainage availability, etc. in totality. In absence of a proper system, we see 8/10 storied buildings being constructed by the side of a 40'/50' (12.19m/15.24m) wide roads, causing heavy traffic jams as a result of the increased movement of people/vehicles in that area.

   Some of the solutions while doing constructions on narrow roads:

   a. Increase parking space and issue proportionate extra F.S.I. to that building to avoid parking problems. Please note: The parking area should be calculated considering the next 25/30 years.

   b. To increase the width of the road in front of these buildings, construct new buildings 10' (3.04m) to 50' (15.24m) away from the roads, and issue the additional F.S.I./T.D.R. to the builders for parking.

   c. Wherever suitable, similar arrangements may be made for the existing buildings also. **E.g.** in some cases, unwanted compound walls may be demolished to increase the road width. Sanctions for additional F.S.I. to a building for parking area can be provided. If this is not possible, these areas can be converted into T.D.R., and the same can be issue somewhere else for *dedicated parking areas*.

   d. Demolish the ground floors of old buildings/structures (excluding columns), and convert them into parking areas. Grant equivalent F.S.I. to construct additional structures on the same building itself. If this is not possible, convert the equivalent area into T.D.R. which can be used elsewhere to construct residential flats/commercial premises.

2. The local government authorities will sanction any plan only after studying all the above points in totality. If all the requirements are not fulfilled in a satisfactory manner, **the permission should not be granted.** In such a case, F.S.I. should be converted into T.D.R. and sanctioned to the builders. It should be ensured that implementation of this T.D.R. is done only at suitable places, **where the above problems will not arise.**

3. It should also be ensured that old buildings are not be demolished quickly to get additional F.S.I or T.D.R. Otherwise, sanctioning of these will result into more congestion on the roads.

4. I.D.P. department has to work very efficiently and professionally. They have a huge task in their hand. This department has to plan for the next 25/30 years. Availability of space is one major issue; however, they also have to consider the roads, parking places and drainage systems, etc. around the new constructions.

34. **Driving License System:** This needs to be streamlined and strengthened completely. The **new road and transport planning of entire India** will include teaching people the basics and discipline of driving/traffic. There will be written/oral/practical exams. Every physically fit citizen of India can apply for a license at the age of 16. Hence these lessons may be taught right from schools and colleges. These exams will be applicable even for the renewal of expired licenses.

35. **Toll:** The following system should be adopted at all toll booths:
   a. Information on 'the length and width of road for which the toll is collected, the order value of that work, toll period, start and finish date of the toll, collected toll and balance payment details, etc., should be displayed on electronic boards near the toll booths at all times. Other detailed information should also be available in case someone wishes to enquire about the same. Toll collection period will be 2 to 4/5 years maximum depending upon the construction cost. There will be no increase in toll rates till the end. Transparency in the transactions is compulsory.
   b. Separate lanes for people paying by credit cards/electronic payments.

c. The distance between two toll stations will be at least 50 km.

d. In case of traffic jams, regularizing the traffic will be the top priority for the toll booth management. Any vehicle that cannot move on within 5 minutes causes a traffic jam which needs to be cleared. These jams will be cleared on priority before resuming the toll collection again.

In this way, with minimum changes and in the shortest time, we can standardize the road structure in entire India and regularize the traffic economically.

36. **Important Matter:** At present, there is no proper system for the people to realize national problems or issues neatly. While implementing anything that is new, people need to be educated about it first without which the plan will not be successful. Hence, people should be instructed/guided about new suggestions/system systematically. **E.g.** It is necessary to display the rules/regulations with proper illustrations at the beginning of every road. Such display boards will be placed at regular intervals on all roads. On highways and major roads those can be placed 25 to 50 km apart.

Other display boards concerning social issues, safety related matters, etc. may also be installed.

Some suggestions to educate people:

a. 80% advertisement plan: Wherever there is an advertisement (e.g. on roads, buildings, etc.), 20% of space of the same will be allotted to the country for social cause, planning, solutions, etc. None of the advertisement will be 100% of the respective product or the company. **E.g.** If one is travelling on a 50' (15.24m) wide city road, there will be hoardings on the roadside in which 20% space will display 50' (15.24m) wide road sketch and 80% space will show product of the company. Just outside of the I.D.P. fast track court, 20% space of the hoardings will display court rules and regulations, while on some hoardings, information about various departments shall be shown. 80% advertisement plan will be same in all cities, villages and throughout the nation.

b. Local Grampanchayat/corporation/state/central government authorities can utilize some space/time from the newspapers/ TV/Radio/Mobile phone coverage for social issues. These issues may also be added in the respective syllabus to create an early awareness among the children.

c. 'Fine System' wills also being strengthened so that people get a proper sense of right and wrong. **E.g.** parking of vehicles in 'no parking areas', breaking lane system, doing business on the roads although **'Chota Parivar'** is ready, not implementing I.D.P. fast track court's decision, etc. For all such crime, there will be maximum fine and minimum punishment. I.D.P. department will take all responsibilities and will prepare new rules, regulations and systems.

d. The details of all these fines and punishments will be displayed on hoardings, on radio/TV and will be published in newspapers. Due to this, people will follow rules and regulations and will have discipline.

Point **a** and **b** mentioned above are neither compulsory nor penal. However, **whatever good and useful we offer to the society will have its positive results in due course and vice versa,** hence we will dedicate 20% time/space for **revival of India.**

37. **Making funds available to Revive India':**—Even though there are insufficient funds for the development, there is no point in increasing taxes. As a matter of fact, 'abolition of Taxes' is one of the main focus areas of **Arthakranti.** In this case we need to avoid taking new loans from the World Bank/IMF/other countries for raising funds. India and many other countries are already under pressure of existing loans. Our government had introduced B.O.T. (Built-Operate-Transfer) Plan to construct new roads for the last few years. As a result some roads were constructed and a 'Toll' system was started.

In principle, this was a very useful and practical system. However, it gave rise to huge corruption due to lack of control and transparency on the Toll Booths. Collecting more toll than the approved amount has become a routine on toll booths nowadays, and in many cases the collection continues even after the initial expenses are recovered. This even caused agitations against the Toll Booths. **Shri. Bandamaharaj Karadkar and his team** investigated and found out that Rs. 305 crores were collected through the toll near Pune against the Rs. 105crores basic construction value. **How will revive India** if such a huge siphoning of funds is going on? How will the new roads plans be successfully executed? Hence, instead of BOT plan, we will follow the procedure of **'Konkan Railway Shares'** and bonds. **E.g.** If Pune Municipal Corporation/local development government organizations wish to plan a complete development structure of the city/village along with the IDP department for the next 10-15 years, a huge amount will be required for development of the road infrastructure alone. In the new system, the local authorities can raise funds through shares and bonds, etc. for that project. Since these amounts will be invested in **revival of India**, the government can offer 2% more interest to the investors compared to market rates. Thus, the funds can be generated for each new development plan. The funds generation will be like this: Funds Generated from Shares/Bonds = Estimated Value of the Project - Available Government funds for the project. In this way, local government authorities can complete the new development rapidly with high quality outcome with IDP department in the available funds. The benefits to investors are as below:

a. Since the entire investment will be with the government, the funds will be 100% secure and people will get 2% higher interest than market rates.

b. The biggest benefit of investors will be that they can actually witness the developments being made with their own funds. This will generate tremendous self respect and confidence on the government.

So, people will invest right from local to national development plans. After completion of the respective road developments, local government department can collect the minimum toll for some years **(from 2 to 4/5 years)** with full transparency. Toll rates will be constant till end. Local government Departments also can collect monthly rent forest abolishing new water/drainage lines as well. This type of funds management can be adopted in villages on a smaller scale where finance is not available.

In this manner, other cities, where investment and expenses are high, will also develop very fast and independently. (How can we forget the response to 'Konkan Railway Shares/Bonds?')

If any local government can assure transparency for the estimation, duration, facilities available to people (e.g. water, road, light, etc.), and the interest amount they will receive, **I am confident that small villages will also develop independently in the next 8/10 years.** There is no need to send our money through taxes (direct and indirect) to the Central Government, only 10-15% from which will reach us for development. This is the most corrupt system in our country. It will vanish automatically after implementation of **'Arthakranti'** plan. If 'Arthakranti' plan is introduced in totality, a huge amount of money will be generated and collected in the entire country, and then India will become a **'Golden Sparrow'** in the next 15/20 years. Hence we have to join hands together with the local/state/central government departments, and invest our funds in the local/state/central development plans as per our choice.

If govt. has developed some rules/regulations for this type of fund management and government systems wish to work on it, a micro-level investment structures can be developed rapidly with the IDP department.

Frequently Asked Questions

1. Various plans exist with the government/local corporation/administration departments. What is new in this I.D.P. department?
   Answer: I.D.P. department is aglow up of patriotic people in which you and I can contribute and can execute the projects from concept to completion independently in the interest of the nation. This thought process gives it a new dimension even though it is not prepared by professional organizations/experts who charge huge fees.

2. Is there a possibility that the I.D.P. department along with these5 teams also turn into a **'Government Department'** in future?
   Answer: To avoid this, the I.D.P. department will be formed separately. People who have been working on similar projects for the past 10-12 years will be part of this department. These people will be highly motivated and willing to do something in the interest of the nation. Examinations will be conducted to assess the minimum required caliber for the people joining this department, whose overall functioning will be more like a private limited/limited organization than a Government-run enterprise. The Government/local administrative departments will look after only two things:
   1. IDP department's administrative expenses and funds for the implementation of the Plans.
   2. Complete documentation such as objections of people, pastrecords, Government approvals, necessary permissions, etc. Apart from these, the entire responsibility to complete the projects will be of IDP department. In the present situation, we cannot suggest anything to the government departments.

We cannot take part in execution nor can we guide them. The new IDP department will not repeat these and similar mistakes. The IDP department will understand the problems thoroughly and will work for the people, with the people along with related Government departments.

3. In this planning, certain drastic changes will be required, such as new teams for road planning, formation of IDP fast track courts, etc., which seems an impossible task.

   Answer: Please note that there are sizeable changes required for all mega projects. Still Government is interested in megaprojects such as METROs, SKYWALKs, Bus Rapid Transit (B.R.T.), bullet trains, etc. although the success of these projects is still questionable. Why? Instead of this, if we hand over the responsibility to the I.D.P. department, many practical projects will get completed in lesser time and with smaller investments. We will have to work sincerely and towards a common goal with I.D.P. departments rather than investing huge time and money in unrealistic megaprojects.

4. In this planning, the width of the footpaths seems very less. What is the provision for people riding bicycles?

   Answer: We have considered the minimum required width for footpaths as shown in the sketches. If required, the width of footpaths may be increased up to nearby shops/houses/compound walls depending on the situation. After ensuring the required standard width of the roads, footpaths may be widened from 3' (0.91m) to 30' (9.1m) depending on the space availability and the number of people on it. Bicycle tracks may be made along the footpaths as shown on **page no. 90.** The cycle track width can be kept from 3' (0.91m) to 10' (3.04m) as per the local situation. Where separate cycle tracks are not available, cycles can travel in the lanes for two-wheelers.

5. What will be done in cities when the road width is 155' (47.26m)? What is the plan for cities when the road width is more than 200' (60.97m)?

   Answer: We have already shown 100' (30.49m) wide one-way and two-way city roads. Two-way roads of width 120' (36.58m) to 200' (60.97m) wide are also shown. Hence, convert 155' (47.26m) wide city road into a 160' (48.78m) wide city road. Other roads also can be standardized in the same manner.

For roads more than 200' (60.97m) wide, follow 'expressways' only, because crossing of 200' (60.97m) wide roads is risky for the pedestrians. Hence, we will try to follow 'expressway' standardization for wider roads.

6. What can be done if there are 28' (8.54m) or 32' (9.76m) wide one-way roads in a city where city buses are not required?

   Answer: While following standardization, small changes can be done. In this case, form 7' (2.13m) wide parking lane at one side, and follow the 20' (6.1m) or 25' (7.62m) wide standard road.

7. What should be done if continuous parking is not required on 50'/60' (15.24m/18.29m) wide roads? Also, what is the resolution when both side parking is required on 30' (9.14m) wide roads?

   Answer: You can change the transportation planning as per the local requirements. e.g. You can increase two-wheeler lanes or you can have parking on both sides. Refer to some exceptional situations on **page no. 83 to 90.** Please also refer to parking standardization on **page no. 91 to 94.** However, while making other changes, one should not deviate from the standardizations such as width of parking lane, width of two-wheeler/four-wheeler lanes, width of the roads, bus stop markings, zebra crossing markings, signal system, etc. It will be necessary to follow the sketches.

8. What will be the effect of this planning on unemployment and environmental issues?

   Answer: Protecting environment basically means we should get fresh air to breathe. However, we usually do nothing unless breathing becomes impossible due to pollution. This planning will have 'environment' as a core issue. Millions of subsequent opportunities will be generated for the people who wish to work in this field.

9. Why should the Government listen to our plans and implement the same?

   Answer: We are simplifying the work for the Government by offering them readymade, cost effective and practical solutions. Once our people are convinced about the usefulness of this planning, no government can ignore it, as it is in the best interest of the nation.

10. Should we carry on with projects like metros, skywalks, monorails, B.R.T.'s? Are we for the development or not?

Answer: We need to carry on with such developments; however certain things need to be kept in mind. **E.g.** In Pune, the skywalk project has been estimated at approx. Rs. 25 crore/km. Skywalk is an elevated footpath at a height of 18' (5.5m) with approx. 3m widthand4.5km length. This skywalk will be built at one end of the main city road. The total investment for this will be approx. Rs.113/- crore.

If we try to judge the benefits of this skywalk as compared to the cost of this project, anyone can imagine how impracticable this project will be.

If we imagine that 100 km long footpaths (actually these are very less) will be required in Pune seeing the population and rush, then investment **will be Rs. 25 crore per km x 100 km = Rs. 2500 crore, only for footpath!** Is it really worth investing Rs. 2,500/- crore on a hi-tech footpath in one city of India? How much **'CHOTA PARIWAR'** units can be built in this investment? And in that case, all the roadside hawkers can sell their products easily without the fear of the police or local government. They can have a better standard of living. That way, the footpaths will be empty automatically. This is one of the examples why we need to set our priorities right and work towards our goal in a systematic and methodical manner.

On the other hand, local citizens are well aware about their needs and problems, and they can solve those in minimum time and expenses. **Precisely this is the main object of I.D.P. department.** We all have to understand the same and think over it deeply. We have to execute the plans of I.D.P. departments on top priority. Definitely, we will build all the above big projects. But before that we must simplify the life of people very fast and economically. **This is real progress!**

People's Responsibilities/Contribution Along with the Government

1. We will understand the sketches/standardization and will help the local government officers/staff accordingly. We will give the permission to demolish the buildings/structures obstructing the

construction/widening of roads. We will make sure that all the roads/ open spaces are tarred upto our structure, compound, building, shop, house, etc.

2. Wherever possible (like in housing societies, industrial areas, commercial buildings, etc.) we will come together and standardize the internal roads. We will make sure that these roads have tar on it. If we have open gutters in front of the houses, we will install drainage pipe lines so that the whole road becomes wide.

3. All types of rules (new as well as old) will be followed by us and will prove ourselves. We will park the vehicles in parking areas only. People will use the public transportation as much as possible. The pedestrians will walk only on footpaths and not on the roads. Discipline to form and follow a queue system at bus stop will be practiced. We will maintain cleanliness on bus stops, buses, railway stations, roads, etc. This will develop self respect and respect for the country in due course. This will have a tremendous impact on fuel consumption and economy of the country.

4. The pedestrians will cross the roads only on zebra crossing and all the drivers will give priority to pedestrians to cross.

   We will break the habit of crossing the roads on wrong sides/at any time/anywhere. We will break all the bad habits such as driving on wrong side, stopping anywhere on the road and interrupting the traffic, spitting, littering, unnecessary horn blowing, etc.

5. Pedestrians will walk on one side (left side) in places like bus stops, railway stations, bus stands, footpaths, zebra crossings and wherever possible.

6. For the nation, if required, sufficient place will be provided to build bus stops.

7. At present our transport system is extremely weak in villages. This puts a strain on private and public transportation. According to the new system, village people will travel in shared big/small taxies & micro/mini bus. However, the number of passengers will be as per the exact specified capacity of the respective vehicle. Hence local government will issue sufficient additional licenses so that total number of transport vehicles will be increased. **Secondly school auto**

rickshaw/vans/buses will be manufactured with a different design as shown on page no. 178 to 182.

Some additional important rules regarding the new road and transportation system:

1. Since lane system will be marked compulsory on each and every road, taking a turn as per the driver's whim will not be allowed. It will be allowed only at a signal/U-turn/wherever mentioned. Pedestrians will be allowed to cross the roads only on zebra crossings. All the vehicles have to follow the lane system and the rules, otherwise heavy fine will be applicable to all. A vehicle will be allowed to get out of the lane only at the time of overtaking.

2. **Information of markings:**
   a. White markings (broken) : Marking for two-wheelers, cars, LCVs, big vehicles
   b. Red Marking : Marking for 'city buses' inside the city limits
   : Emergency lane on expressways.
   c. Yellow Marking:
   (Inside city limits) : Two-wheeler/four-wheeler parking
   (Outside city limits) : Two-wheeler lane
   d. White Marking
   (Continuous) : The middle part of the road and end
   e. Green Marking : Dividers

3. **Parking:** All the vehicles such as two-wheelers, cars, rickshaw, buses, trucks, etc. will be parked parallel in parking lane. Heavy fines will be charged for people who violate the rules. Please refer the sketches on **page no. 91 to 94.** Two vehicles will be parked according to the new parking system, like two buses/ two cars/two taxis/two or four rickshaws and four two-wheelers. 7' (2.13m for car/rickshaw) and 15' (4.57m for bus/truck) of space will be left in front and at the back so that parking becomes easy. There will be three types of parking system for two-wheelers. **Two-wheelers Left parking as per page no. 91 and Two-wheeler Right parking as per page no. 92.**

4. P-1/P-2 type 'Parking' system is very inconvenient and unsafe. Hence, it will be discontinued in the whole country. While accepting this new 'parking system', the new 'parking areas' will also be made available.

5. The over-bridges, parking areas, etc., that are available now will remain. But we can try to standardize them. Remember that all the new over bridges, subways, all types of roads, expressways, highways, etc., will be constructed as per the standard design. After the standardization of main roads, the leftover space may be used for other roads/service roads. Existing roads, parking, dividers, footpath can be converted to the nearest standardization.

6. Crossing the expressways shall be prohibited. There will be a continuous divider which will restrict people from crossing these expressways. Over bridges/subways will be introduced for crossing, left/right or U-turning. All the over-bridges constructed on expressways will have the minimum clear height of 20' (6.1m). This rule will be made mandatory and will be applicable for all the over-bridges in the country.

7. Unauthorized vehicles using the emergency lane will be charged a fine of **Rs. 1965/-** per vehicle. This fine will be valid for 20 km only. The same type of fine will be applicable for the vehicles not keeping their lanes. All the ambulances, fire engines, cranes to clear accident vehicles, etc. will travel in the emergency lane. No other vehicle will be permitted to use this lane including vehicles of celebrities. Automatic cameras on regular intervals will be installed for controlling the above and ensuring that all rules are followed.

8. Similarly any violation in traffic rules resulting fine of Rs. **1965/-** Insurance Company also follow the same rule at the time of renewal of policy. The boards/stones mentioning of **1965** will be displayed on city road/state/high ways/expressways at an intervals in such fashion that people will respect the figure of **1965** & will follow self discipline.

9. There will be checking of vehicles and the drivers at every 4/5th toll booth to avoid accidents. The checking will be restricted to good vehicular brakes and sobriety of the driver.

10. Every driver has to complete the syllabus in driving school. This syllabus will include written, oral and practical exam. A new syllabus will be designed for this on the basis of '**New road & transport planning of entire India.**

ABSTRACT

Infrastructure Development Plan—I.D.P. (With Active Teams)

IDP Fast Track Court	Road Width Team	Leveled Road Team	Parking Area Team	Chota Pariwar Team
A. All decisions will be made within 8/9 weeks. **B.** There will be no provision for stay orders or delays. **C.** First priority will be given to building of roads in a proper manner and simplicity in transportation. **D.** Fast decisions for rehabilitation and supervision of the same up to completion. **E.** Special powers for rehabilitation e.g. Proper valuation, issuing of additional FSI.	**A.** The width of the roads should be the same in all the cities. Standardization of all roads and assured completion of work. **B.** Supervision of road work till the completion. **C.** Continuous and fast track communication with the IDP department. **D.** The entire road width should be tarred up to the adjoining shops, houses, footpaths, etc. **E.** Similarly work on outer cities. **F.** All bus stops should be standardized.	**A.** Major work is leveling of all roads, footpaths, etc. For this, remove all hurdles. **B.** All manhole covers should be leveled. **C.** Continuous repairs of all potholes. There should not be any ups-and-downs on the roads. **D.** Convert open gutters (Nalla) into closed pipeline in villages/cities. **E.** Remove all the speed breakers. **F.** All cycle tracks, footpaths should be clean and open for the traffic.	**A.** Create common parking places at every 2/3 km. in cities/towns/villages. **B.** For these, make 2 to 7/8 storied parking buildings depending upon requirement. **C.** Maintain all other parking areas of the city and educate people about the same. **D.** Make and maintain the parking lanes/markings on the roads. Wherever applicable, write the standardized specifications. **E.** Make and maintain all zebra crossings.	**A.** Understand people's problems solve them and educate them. **B.** Make and maintain 'Chota Pariwar' buildings at every 1.5 to 2 km. depending upon the demand. These buildings can be 2 to 7/8 storied depending upon the need and situation. **C.** Build the Pariwar in totality and supervise continuously. **D.** Make sure that no one does business on footpaths/roads. **E.** Responsibility to make sure that all roads and footpaths area l ways clear for smooth transportation.

F. No facility of high/ supreme court appeals. **G.** Quick decision for demolishing of buildings for road widening.			**F.** Keep an eye on parked vehicles to ensure that they all are in the parking area or in the parking lane.	

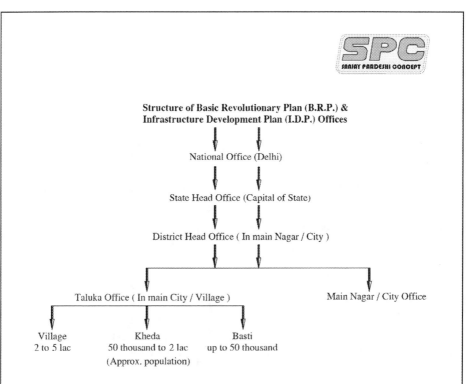

Structure of Basic Revolutionary Plan (B.R.P.) &
Infrastructure Development Plan (I.D.P.) Offices

National Office (Delhi)

State Head Office (Capital of State)

District Head Office (In main Nagar / City)

Taluka Office (In main City / Village)   Main Nagar / City Office

Village   Kheda   Basti
2 to 5 lac   50 thousand to 2 lac   up to 50 thousand
                    (Approx. population)

The big question : What type of people will be in BRP & IDP departments...?

Answer : Specialists, businessmen, administrators, technocrats, staff, officers, thinkers, researchers, people with a creative mind and every patriotic person will join an open forum called **'How to Revive India..?'** Some people will be in BRP & IDP departments.

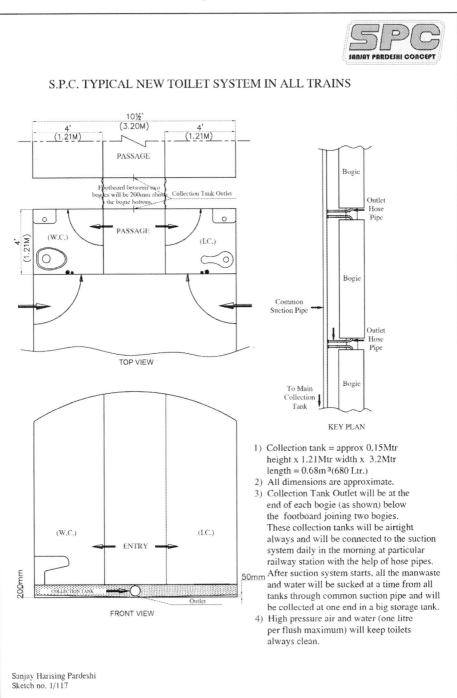

S.P.C. TYPICAL NEW TOILET SYSTEM IN ALL TRAINS

1) Collection tank = approx 0.15Mtr height x 1.21Mtr width x 3.2Mtr length = $0.68m^3$(680 Ltr.)
2) All dimensions are approximate.
3) Collection Tank Outlet will be at the end of each bogie (as shown) below the footboard joining two bogies. These collection tanks will be airtight always and will be connected to the suction system daily in the morning at particular railway station with the help of hose pipes. After suction system starts, all the manwaste and water will be sucked at a time from all tanks through common suction pipe and will be collected at one end in a big storage tank.
4) High pressure air and water (one litre per flush maximum) will keep toilets always clean.

Sanjay Harising Pardeshi
Sketch no. 1/117

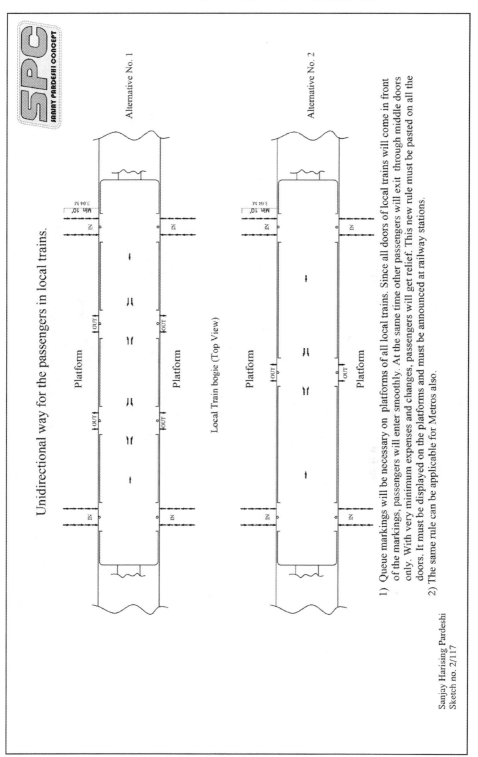

Unidirectional way for the passengers in local trains.

Alternative No. 1

Platform

Platform

Local Train bogie (Top View)

Alternative No. 2

Platform

Platform

1) Queue markings will be necessary on platforms of all local trains. Since all doors of local trains will come in front of the markings, passengers will enter smoothly. At the same time other passengers will exit through middle doors only. With very minimum expenses and changes, passengers will get relief. This new rule must be pasted on all the doors. It must be displayed on the platforms and must be announced at railway stations.

2) The same rule can be applicable for Metros also.

Sanjay Harising Pardeshi
Sketch no. 2/117

49

Unidirectional way for the passengers in local trains (In new type of Second Class bogie)

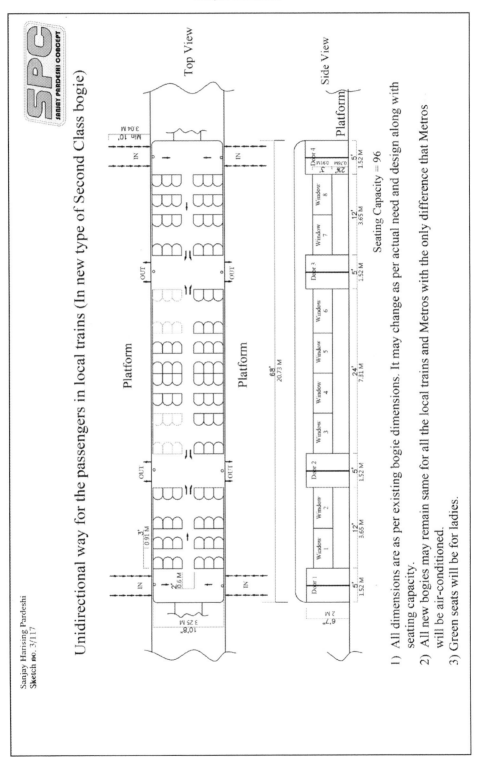

Sanjay Harising Pardeshi
Sketch no. 3/117

Top View

Side View

Platform

Seating Capacity = 96

1) All dimensions are as per existing bogie dimensions. It may change as per actual need and design along with seating capacity.

2) All new bogies may remain same for all the local trains and Metros with the only difference that Metros will be air-conditioned.

3) Green seats will be for ladies.

Unidirectional way for the passengers in local trains (In new type of First Class bogie)

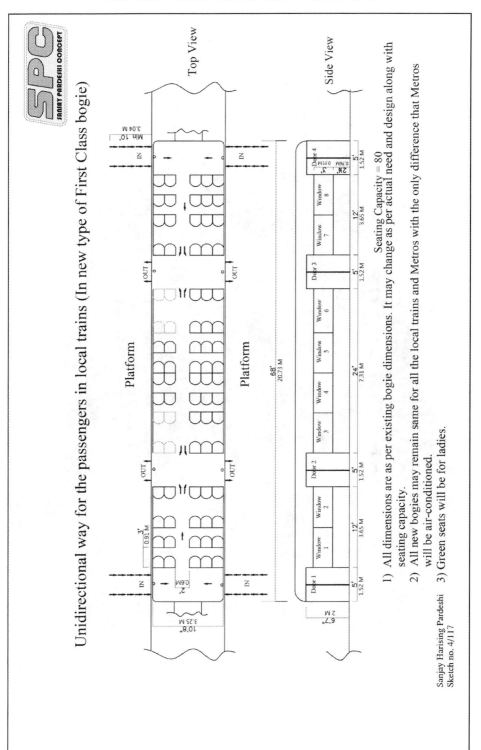

Top View

Side View

Seating Capacity = 80

1) All dimensions are as per existing bogie dimensions. It may change as per actual need and design along with seating capacity.

2) All new bogies may remain same for all the local trains and Metros with the only difference that Metros will be air-conditioned.

3) Green seats will be for ladies.

Sanjay Harising Pardeshi
Sketch no. 4/117

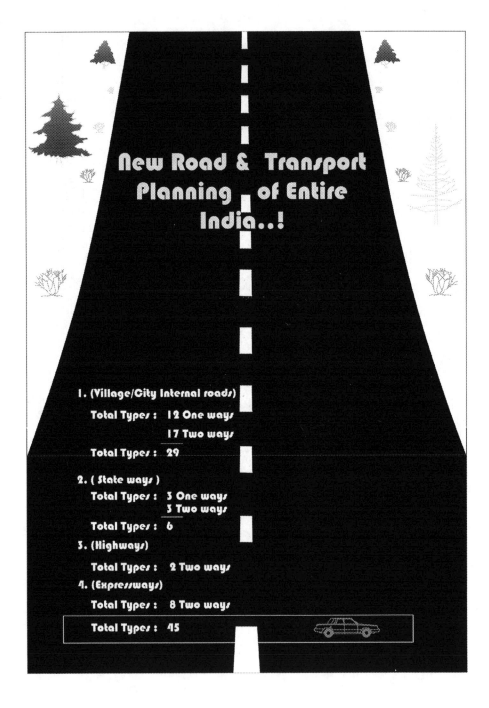

New Road & Transport Planning of Entire India..!

1. (Village/City Internal roads)
   Total Types : 12 One ways
                 17 Two ways
   Total Types : 29

2. (State ways)
   Total Types : 3 One ways
                 3 Two ways
   Total Types : 6

3. (Highways)
   Total Types : 2 Two ways

4. (Expressways)
   Total Types : 8 Two ways

Total Types : 45

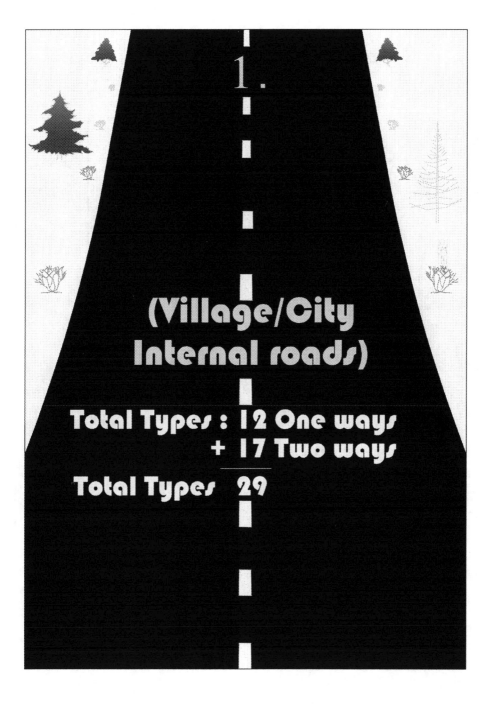

1.

(Village/City Internal roads)

Total Types : 12 One ways
+ 17 Two ways

Total Types   29

S.P.C. 15'(4.57Mtrs.) Wide City Road (One-way)

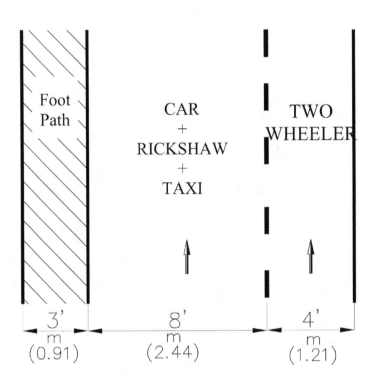

Foot Path

CAR
+
RICKSHAW
+
TAXI

TWO WHEELER

3'
m
(0.91)

8'
m
(2.44)

4'
m
(1.21)

(1) Buses, trucks & mini trucks not allowed.
(2) Due to short road width, parking is not allowed on roads. All vehicles will be parked in parking area.
(3) Due to short width of the road, it is not possible to provide footpaths on both sides.

Sanjay Harising Pardeshi
Sketch no. 5/117

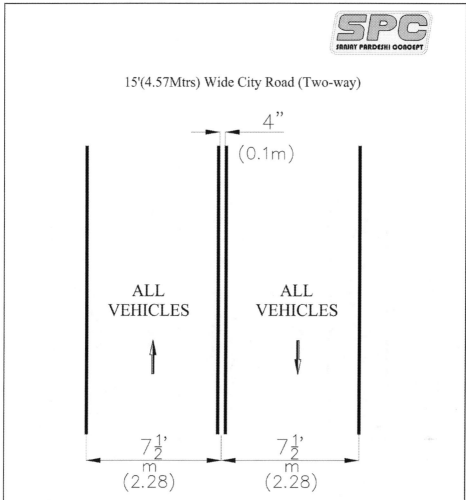

15'(4.57Mtrs) Wide City Road (Two-way)

(1) No Footpath.
(2) Due to short road width, parking is not allowed on roads.
    All vehicles will be parked in parking area.
(3) Buses, trucks & mini trucks not allowed.
(4) Due to short width of the road, it is not possible to provide
    footpaths on both sides.

Sanjay Harising Pardeshi
Sketch no. 6/117

S.P.C. 20'(6.1Mtrs.) Wide City Road (One-way)

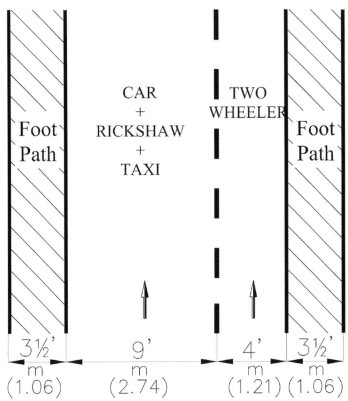

(1) Due to short width of the road, it is not possible to provide footpaths on both sides.

(2) Buses & trucks not allowed.

Sanjay Harising Pardeshi
Sketch no. 7/117

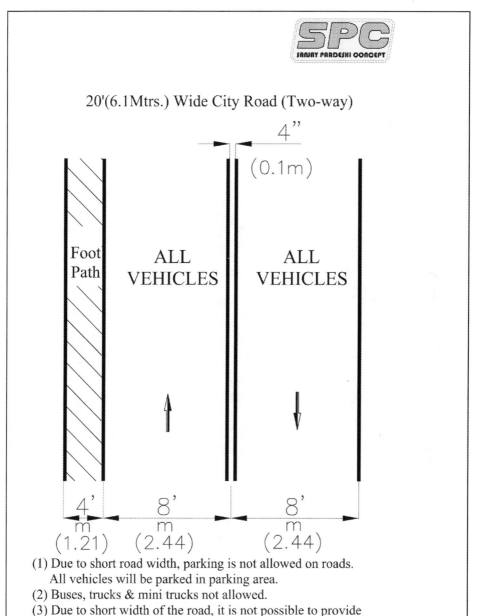

20'(6.1Mtrs.) Wide City Road (Two-way)

(1) Due to short road width, parking is not allowed on roads.
   All vehicles will be parked in parking area.
(2) Buses, trucks & mini trucks not allowed.
(3) Due to short width of the road, it is not possible to provide
   footpaths on both sides

Sanjay Harising Pardeshi
Sketch no. 8/117

S.P.C. 25'(7.62Mtrs.) Wide City Road (One-way)

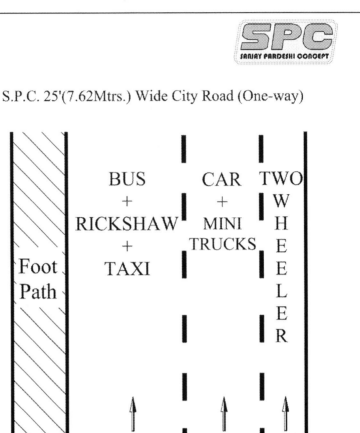

(1) Due to short road width, parking is not allowed on roads. All vehicles will be parked in parking area.
(2) Trucks are not allowed at peak time.
(3) Due to short width of the road, it is not possible to provide footpaths at both side.
(4) Zebra crossing will be at every 0.5 to 0.6 kms. Distance between two bus stop so zebra crossing will be provided at each bus stop as depicted on page no. 123 to 127.

Sanjay Harising Pardeshi
Sketch no. 9/117

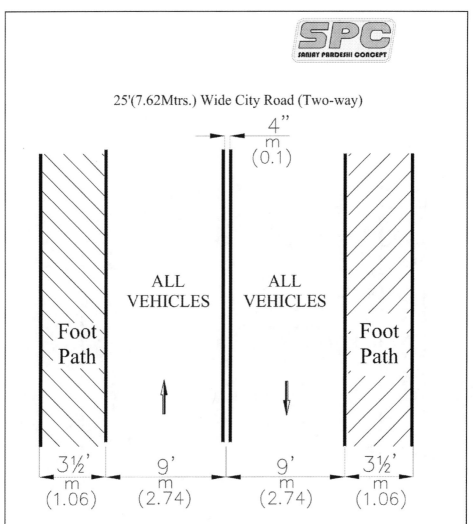

25'(7.62Mtrs.) Wide City Road (Two-way)

4"
m
(0.1)

ALL VEHICLES | ALL VEHICLES

Foot Path

Foot Path

3½' m (1.06)   9' m (2.74)   9' m (2.74)   3½' m (1.06)

(1) Due to short road width, parking is not allowed on roads. All vehicles will be parked in parking area.

(2) Buses and trucks not allowed.

Sanjay Harising Pardeshi
Sketch no. 10/117

S.P.C. 30'(9.14Mtrs.) Wide City Road (One-way)

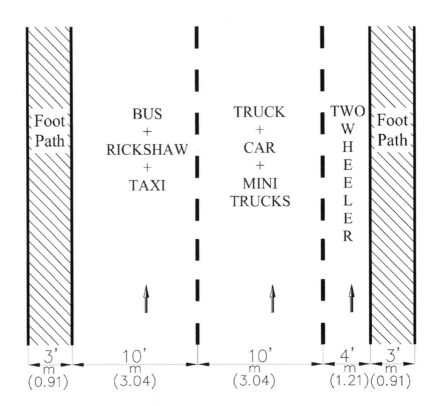

(1) Due to short road width, parking is not allowed on roads.
    All vehicles will be parked in parking area.
(2) Trucks are not allowed at peak time.

Sanjay Harising Pardeshi
Sketch no. 11/117

S.P.C. 30'(9.14Mtrs.) Wide City Road (Two-way)

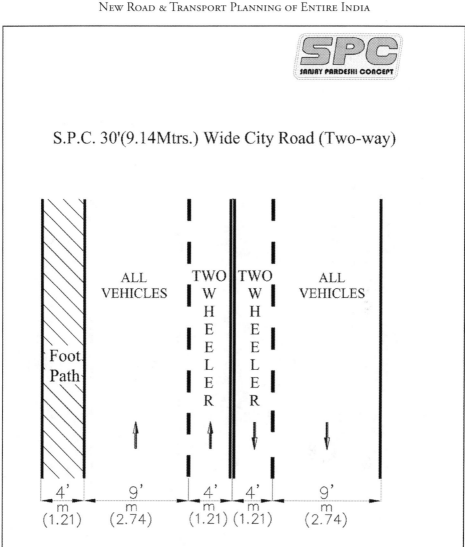

(1) Due to short road width, parking is not allowed on roads. All vehicles will be parked in parking area.
(2) Buses and trucks not allowed.
(3) Due to short width of the road, it is not possible to provide footpaths on both sides.

Sanjay Harising Pardeshi
Sketch no. 12/117

S.P.C. 35'(10.67Mtrs.) Wide City Road (One-way)

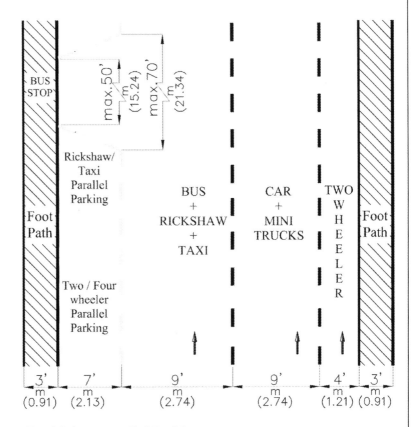

(1) All vehicles - Parallel Parking.
(2) Parking is prohibited at the bus stop.
(3) Trucks are not allowed at peak time.
(4) Vehicles are not allowed in bus lane except auto rickshaw
    and taxies.
(5) Follow parking markings as per the page no. 91, 92, 93 & 94.

Sanjay Harising Pardeshi
Sketch no. 13/117

S.P.C. 35'(10.67Mtrs.) Wide City Road (Two-way)

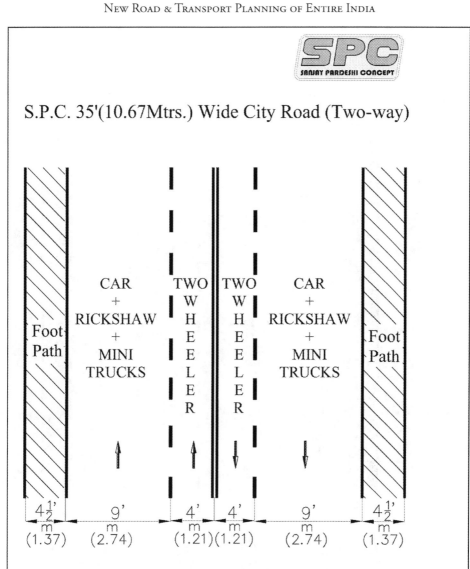

(1) Due to short road width, parking is not allowed on roads. All vehicles will be parked in parking area.

(2) Buses and trucks not allowed.

Sanjay Harising Pardeshi
Sketch no. 14/117

S.P.C. 40'(12.19 Mtrs.) Wide City Road (One-way)

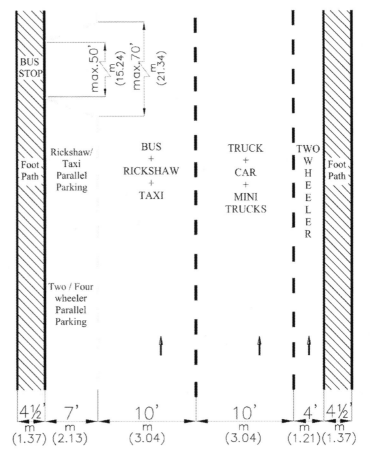

(1) All vehicles - Parallel Parking.
(2) Parking is prohibited at the bus stop.
(3) Trucks are not allowed at peak time.
(4) Vehicles are not allowed in bus lane except auto rickshaw
    and taxies.
(5) Follow parking markings as per the page no. 91, 92, 93 & 94.

Sanjay Harising Pardeshi
Sketch no. 15/117

S.P.C. 40'(12.19 Mtrs.) Wide City Road (Two-way)

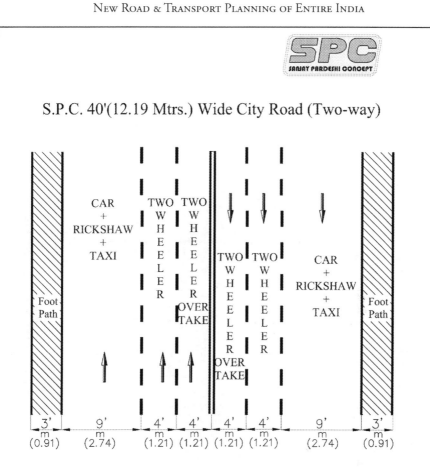

(1) Due to short road width, parking is not allowed on roads. All vehicles will be parked in parking area.

(2) Buses and trucks not allowed.

Sanjay Harising Pardeshi
Sketch no. 16/117

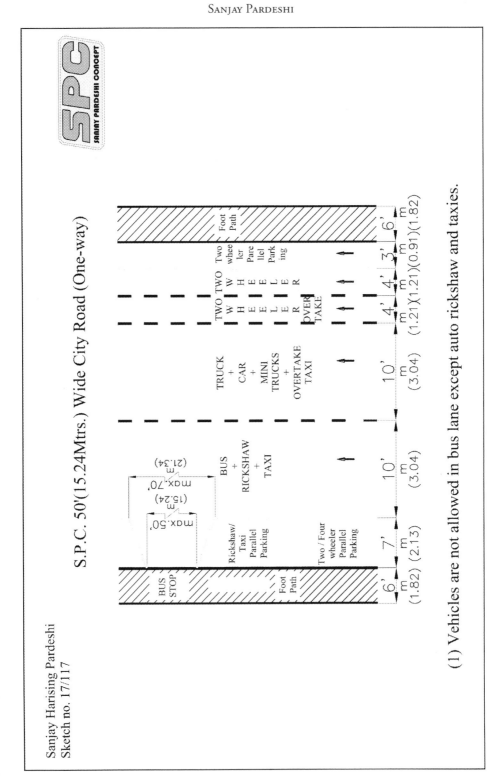

Sanjay Harising Pardeshi
Sketch no. 17/117

S.P.C. 50'(15.24Mtrs.) Wide City Road (One-way)

(1) Vehicles are not allowed in bus lane except auto rickshaw and taxies.

S.P.C. 50'(15.24Mtrs.) Wide City Road (Two-way)

Foot Path	BUS + RICKSHAW + TAXI	CAR + MINI TRUCKS	TWO W H E E L E R	TWO W H E E L E R	CAR + MINI TRUCKS	BUS + RICKSHAW + TAXI	Foot Path
3' m (0.91)	10' m (3.04)	8' m (2.44)	4' m (1.21)	4' m (1.21)	8' m (2.44)	10' m (3.04)	3' m (0.91)

(1) Due to short road width, parking is not allowed on roads. All vehicles will be parked in parking area.

(2) Trucks are not allowed at peak time.

(3) Dividers - will be made from 3"(75mm) pipe (height approx. 3'4"=1M) and will be continuously.

(Typical sketch enclosed page no. 146)

Sanjay Harising Pardeshi
Sketch no. 18/117

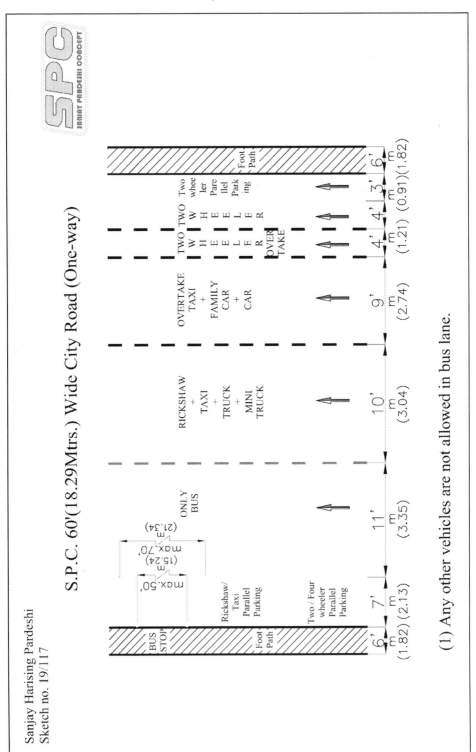

Sanjay Harising Pardeshi
Sketch no. 19/117

S.P.C. 60'(18.29Mtrs.) Wide City Road (One-way)

(1) Any other vehicles are not allowed in bus lane.

S.P.C. 60'(18.29Mtrs.) Wide City Road (Two-way)

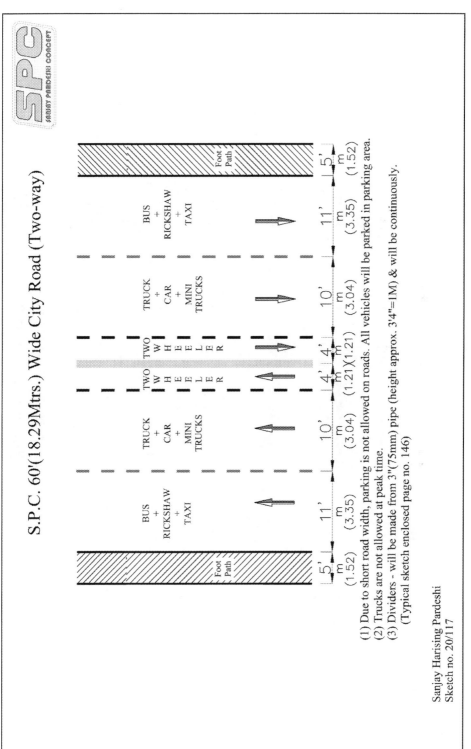

(1) Due to short road width, parking is not allowed on roads. All vehicles will be parked in parking area.
(2) Trucks are not allowed at peak time.
(3) Dividers - will be made from 3"(75mm) pipe (height approx. 3'4"=1M) & will be continuously.
(Typical sketch enclosed page no. 146)

Sanjay Harising Pardeshi
Sketch no. 20/117

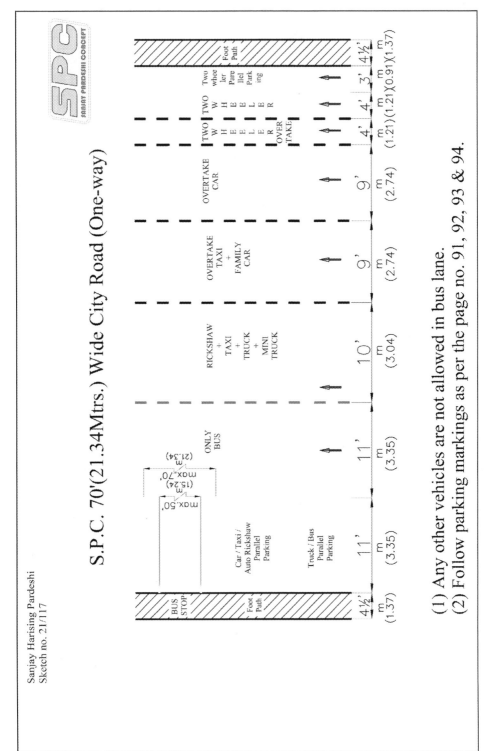

Sanjay Harising Pardeshi
Sketch no. 21/117

S.P.C. 70'(21.34Mtrs.) Wide City Road (One-way)

(1) Any other vehicles are not allowed in bus lane.
(2) Follow parking markings as per the page no. 91, 92, 93 & 94.

S.P.C. 70'(21.34Mtrs.) Wide City Road (Two-way)

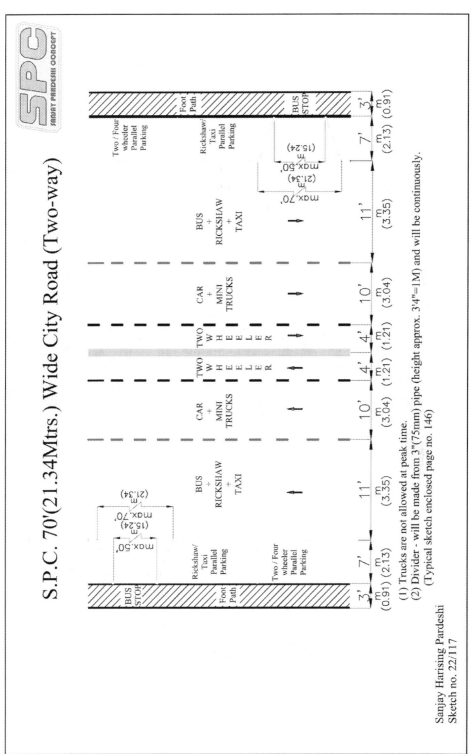

(1) Trucks are not allowed at peak time.
(2) Divider - will be made from 3"(75mm) pipe (height approx. 3'4"=1M) and will be continuously.
    (Typical sketch enclosed page no. 146)

Sanjay Harising Pardeshi
Sketch no. 22/117

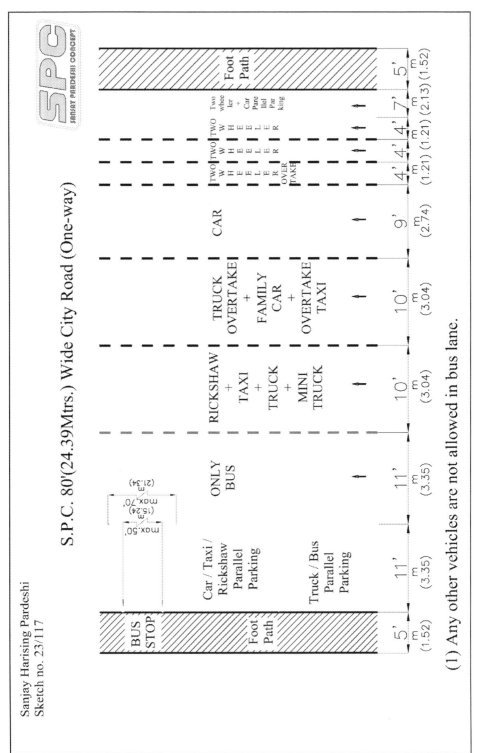

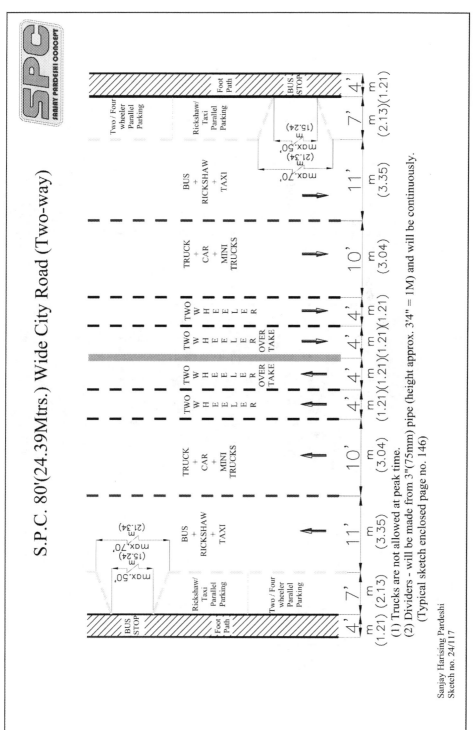

S.P.C. 80'(24.39Mtrs.) Wide City Road (Two-way)

(1) Trucks are not allowed at peak time.
(2) Dividers - will be made from 3"(75mm) pipe (height approx. 3¼" = 1M) and will be continuously.
(Typical sketch enclosed page no. 146)

Sanjay Harising Pardeshi
Sketch no. 24/117

S.P.C. 90'(27.44Mtrs.) Wide City Road (One-way)

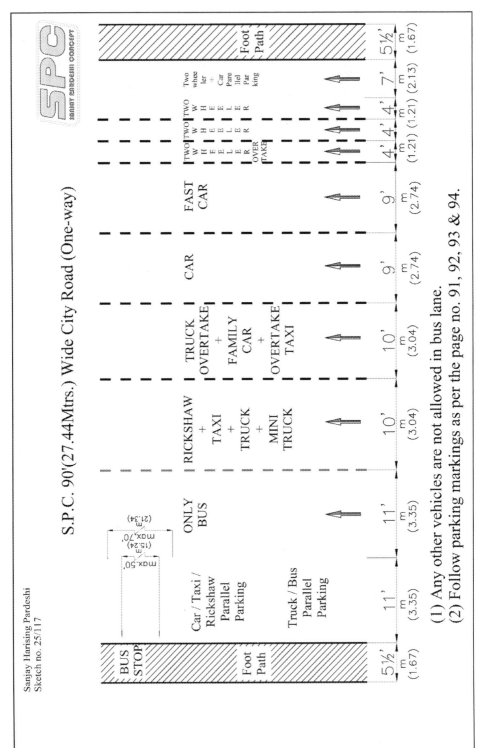

Sanjay Harising Pardeshi
Sketch no. 25/117

(1) Any other vehicles are not allowed in bus lane.
(2) Follow parking markings as per the page no. 91, 92, 93 & 94.

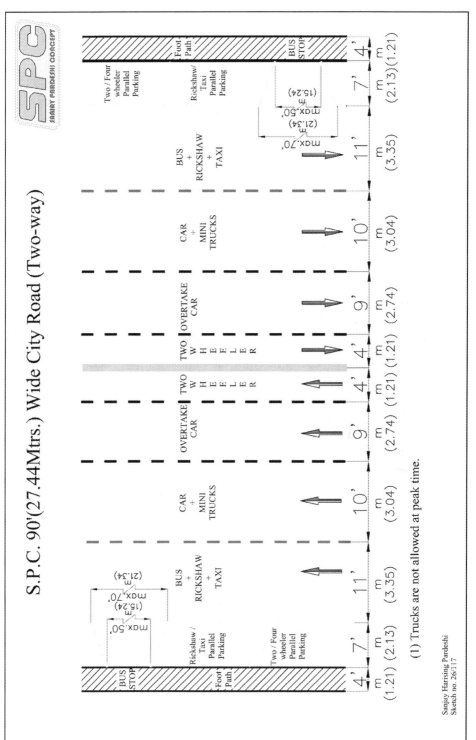

S.P.C. 90'(27.44Mtrs.) Wide City Road (Two-way)

(1) Trucks are not allowed at peak time.

Sanjay Harising Pardeshi
Sketch no. 26/117

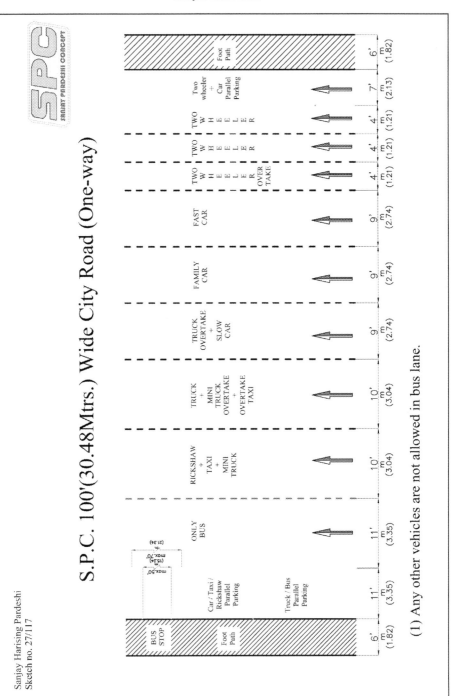

S.P.C. 100'(30.48Mtrs.) Wide City Road (One-way)

Sanjay Harising Pardeshi
Sketch no. 27/117

(1) Any other vehicles are not allowed in bus lane.

S.P.C. 100'(30.48Mtrs.) Wide City Road (Two-way)

(1) Dividers - will be made from 3"(75mm) pipe (height approx. 34" = 1M) and will be continuously.
(Typical sketch enclosed page no. 146)

Sanjay Harising Pardeshi
Sketch no. 28/117

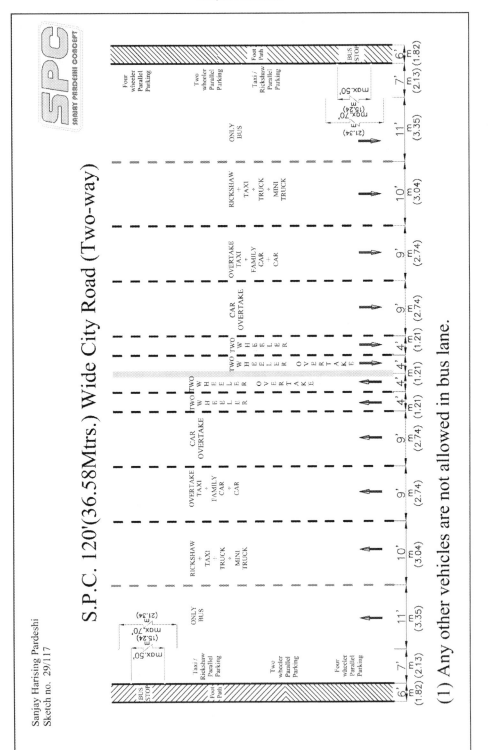

Sanjay Harising Pardeshi
Sketch no. 29/117

S.P.C. 120'(36.58Mtrs.) Wide City Road (Two-way)

(1) Any other vehicles are not allowed in bus lane.

S.P.C. 140'(42.68Mtrs.) Wide City Road (Two-way)

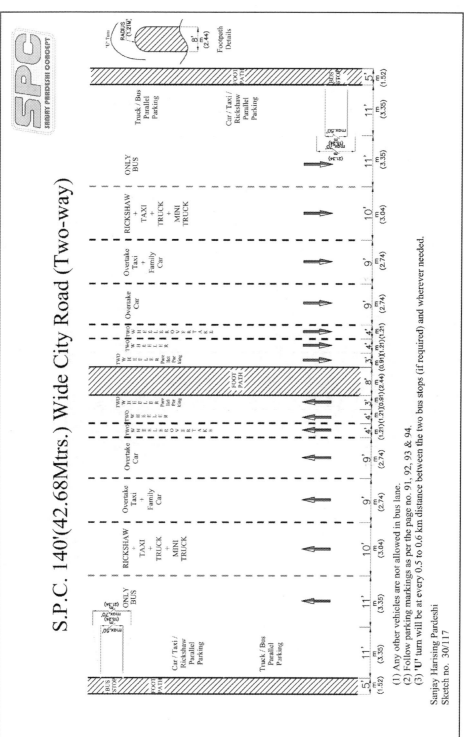

(1) Any other vehicles are not allowed in bus lane.

(2) Follow parking markings as per the page no. 91, 92, 93 & 94.

(3) 'U' turn will be at every 0.5 to 0.6 km distance between the two bus stops (if required) and wherever needed.

Sanjay Harisingh Pardeshi
Sketch no. 30/117

S.P.C. 160'(48.78Mtrs.) Wide City Road (Two-way)

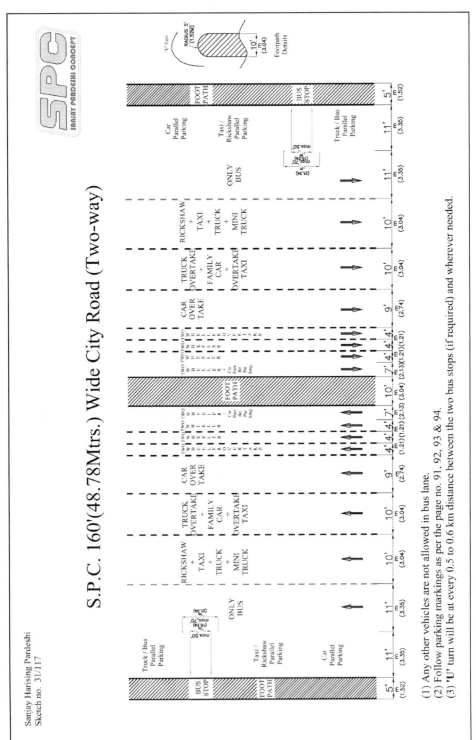

Sanjay Harising Pardeshi
Sketch no. 31/117

(1) Any other vehicles are not allowed in bus lane.
(2) Follow parking markings as per the page no. 91, 92, 93 & 94.
(3) 'U' turn will be at every 0.5 to 0.6 km distance between the two bus stops (if required) and wherever needed.

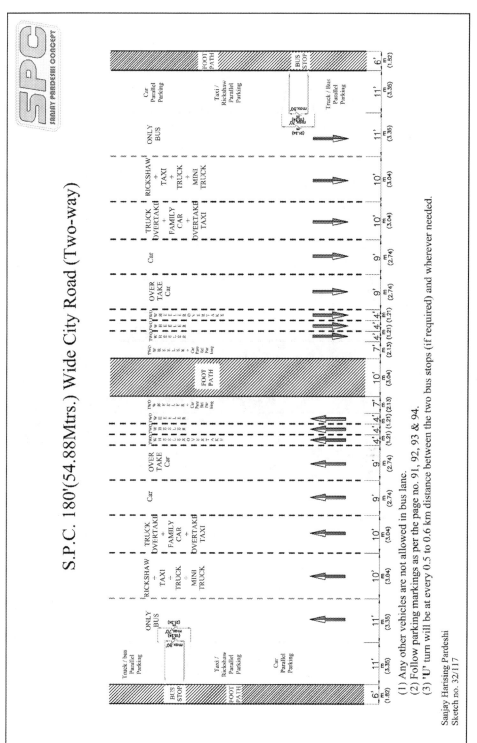

S.P.C. 180'(54.88Mtrs.) Wide City Road (Two-way)

(1) Any other vehicles are not allowed in bus lane.
(2) Follow parking markings as per the page no. 91, 92, 93 & 94.
(3) 'U' turn will be at every 0.5 to 0.6 km distance between the two bus stops (if required) and wherever needed.

Sanjay Harising Pardeshi
Sketch no. 32/117

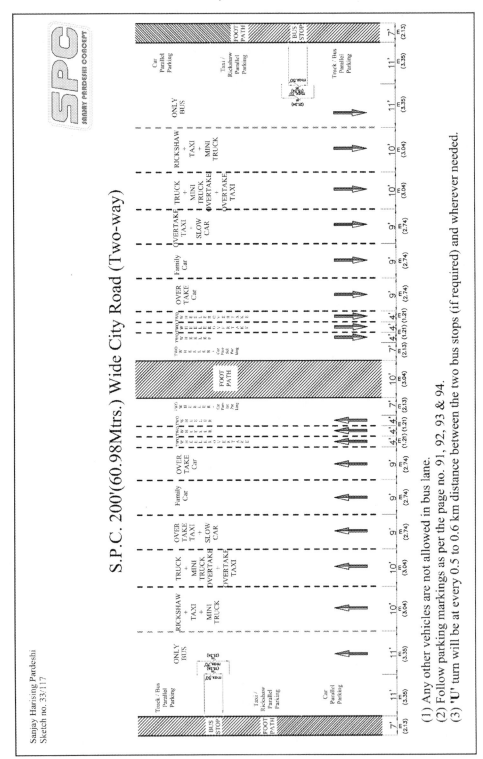

S.P.C. 200'(60.98Mtrs.) Wide City Road (Two-way)

Sanjay Harising Pardeshi
Sketch no. 33'/117

(1) Any other vehicles are not allowed in bus lane.
(2) Follow parking markings as per the page no. 91, 92, 93 & 94.
(3) 'U' turn will be at every 0.5 to 0.6 km distance between the two bus stops (if required) and wherever needed.

Some exceptional situation in city / village
20'(6.1Mtrs.) Wide City Road (One-way)

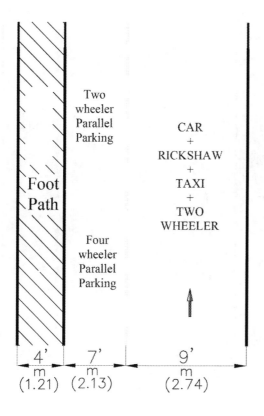

1) Buses & trucks are not allowed.
2) Parking is required.

Sanjay Harising Pardeshi
Sketch no. 34/117

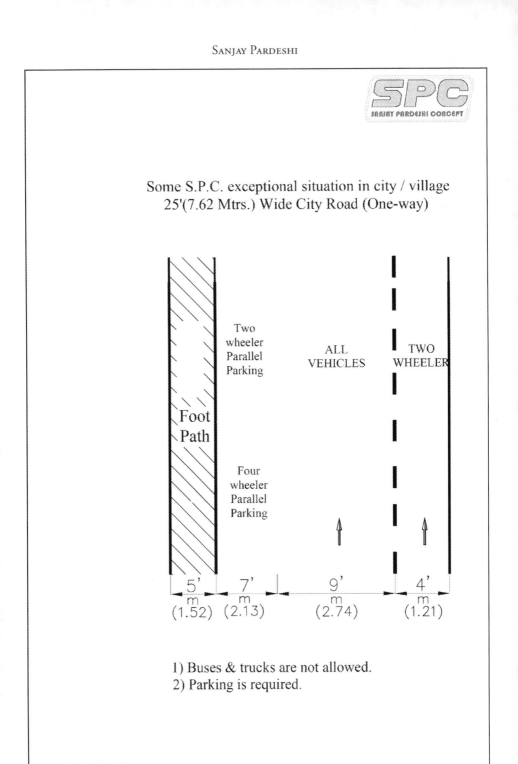

Some S.P.C. exceptional situation in city / village
25'(7.62 Mtrs.) Wide City Road (One-way)

1) Buses & trucks are not allowed.
2) Parking is required.

Sanjay Harising Pardeshi
Sketch no. 35/117

Some S.P.C. exceptional situation in city / village
30'(9.14Mtrs.) Wide City Road (One-way)

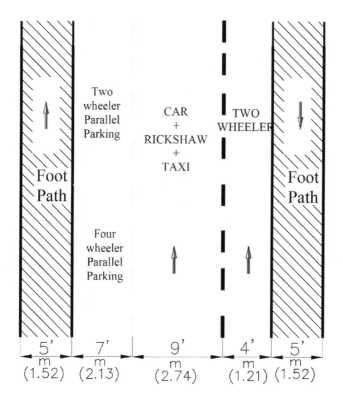

Two wheeler Parallel Parking

CAR + RICKSHAW + TAXI

TWO WHEELER

Foot Path

Foot Path

Four wheeler Parallel Parking

| 5' m (1.52) | 7' m (2.13) | 9' m (2.74) | 4' m (1.21) | 5' m (1.52) |

1) Buses & trucks are not allowed.
2) Footpath is required on both sides because of rush.
3) Parking is required.

Sanjay Harising Pardeshi
Sketch no. 36/117

Some S.P.C. exceptional situation in city / village 35'(10.67 Mtrs.) Wide City Road (One-way)

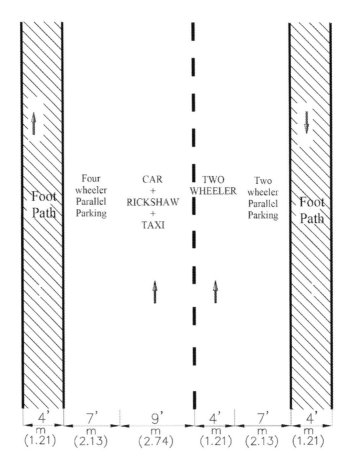

1) Buses & trucks are not allowed.
2) Footpath is required on both sides because of rush.

Sanjay Harising Pardeshi
Sketch no. 37/117

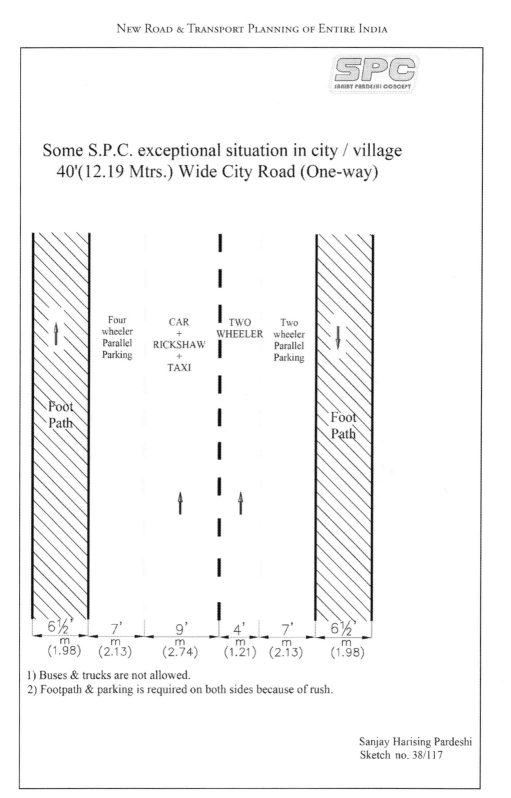

Some S.P.C. exceptional situation in city / village 40'(12.19 Mtrs.) Wide City Road (One-way)

Four wheeler Parallel Parking

CAR + RICKSHAW + TAXI

TWO WHEELER

Two wheeler Parallel Parking

Foot Path

Foot Path

| 6½' m (1.98) | 7' m (2.13) | 9' m (2.74) | 4' m (1.21) | 7' m (2.13) | 6½' m (1.98) |

1) Buses & trucks are not allowed.
2) Footpath & parking is required on both sides because of rush.

Sanjay Harising Pardeshi
Sketch no. 38/117

Some exceptional situation in city / village
20'(6.1Mtrs.) Wide City Road (One-way)

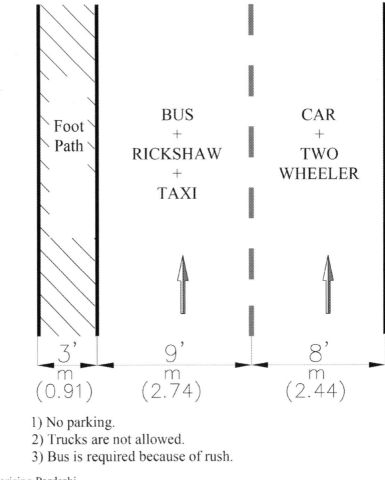

Foot
Path

BUS
+
RICKSHAW
+
TAXI

CAR
+
TWO
WHEELER

3'
m
(0.91)

9'
m
(2.74)

8'
m
(2.44)

1) No parking.
2) Trucks are not allowed.
3) Bus is required because of rush.

Sanjay Harising Pardeshi
Sketch no. 39/117

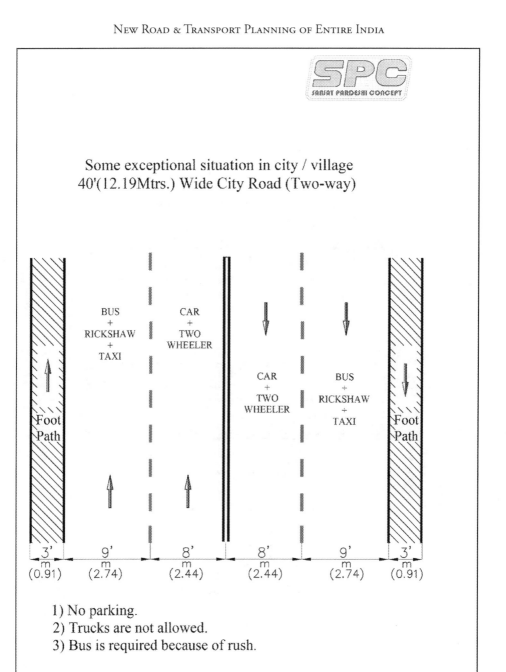

Some exceptional situation in city / village
40'(12.19Mtrs.) Wide City Road (Two-way)

1) No parking.
2) Trucks are not allowed.
3) Bus is required because of rush.

Sanjay Harising Pardeshi
Sketch no. 40/117

TYPICAL S.P.C. 40'(12.19Mtrs) Wide City Road (Two-way)
WITH CYCLE TRACK

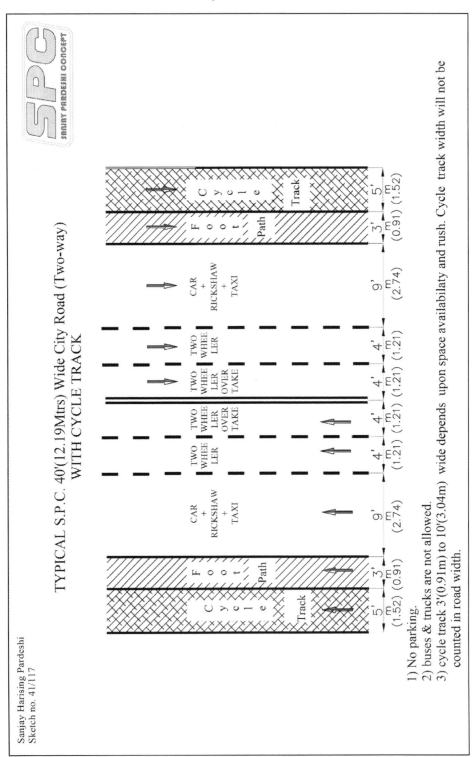

1) No parking.
2) buses & trucks are not allowed.
3) cycle track 3'(0.91m) to 10'(3.04m) wide depends upon space availabilaty and rush. Cycle track width will not be counted in road width.

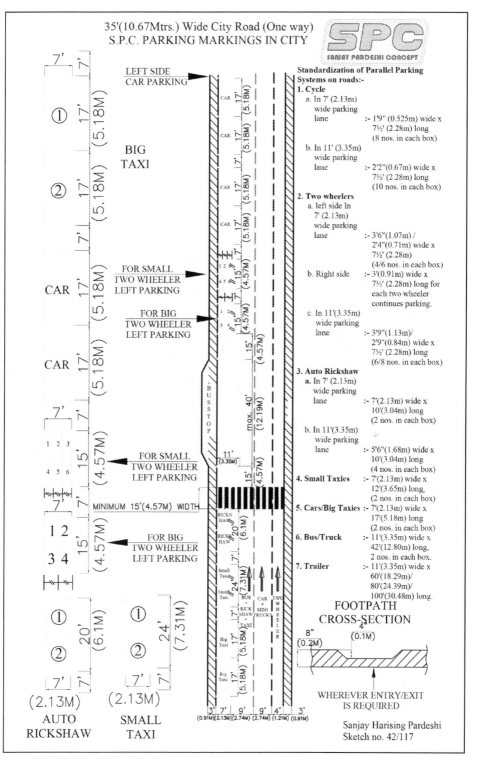

35'(10.67Mtrs.) Wide City Road (One way)
S.P.C. PARKING MARKINGS IN CITY

SPC
SANJAY PARDESHI CONCEPT

LEFT SIDE CAR PARKING

BIG TAXI

CAR

CAR

FOR SMALL TWO WHEELER LEFT PARKING

FOR BIG TWO WHEELER LEFT PARKING

FOR SMALL TWO WHEELER LEFT PARKING

MINIMUM 15'(4.57M) WIDTH

FOR BIG TWO WHEELER LEFT PARKING

AUTO RICKSHAW

SMALL TAXI

Standardization of Parallel Parking Systems on roads:-

1. **Cycle**
   a. In 7' (2.13m) wide parking lane :- 1'9" (0.525) wide x 7½' (2.28m) long (8 nos. in each box)
   b. In 11' (3.35m) wide parking lane :- 2'2"(0.67m) wide x 7½' (2.28m) long (10 nos. in each box)

2. **Two wheelers**
   a. left side In 7' (2.13m) wide parking lane :- 3'6"(1.07m) / 2'4"(0.71m) wide x 7½' (2.28m) (4/6 nos. in each box)
   b. Right side :- 3'(0.91m) wide x 7½' (2.28m) long for each two wheeler continues parking.
   c. In 11'(3.35m) wide parking lane :- 3'9"(1.13m)/ 2'9"(0.84m) wide x 7½' (2.28m) long (6/8 nos. in each box)

3. **Auto Rickshaw**
   a. In 7' (2.13m) wide parking lane :- 7'(2.13m) wide x 10'(3.04m) long (2 nos. in each box)
   b. In 11'(3.35m) wide parking lane :- 5'6"(1.68m) wide x 10'(3.04m) long (4 nos. in each box)

4. **Small Taxies** :- 7'(2.13m) wide x 12'(3.65m) long, (2 nos. in each box)

5. **Cars/Big Taxies** :- 7'(2.13m) wide x 17'(5.18m) long (2 nos. in each box)

6. **Bus/Truck** :- 11'(3.35m) wide x 42'(12.80m) long, 2 nos. in each box.

7. **Trailer** :- 11'(3.35m) wide x 60'(18.29m)/ 80'(24.39m)/ 100'(30.48m) long.

FOOTPATH CROSS-SECTION

8" (0.2M)   (0.1M)

WHEREVER ENTRY/EXIT IS REQUIRED

Sanjay Harising Pardeshi
Sketch no. 42/117

91

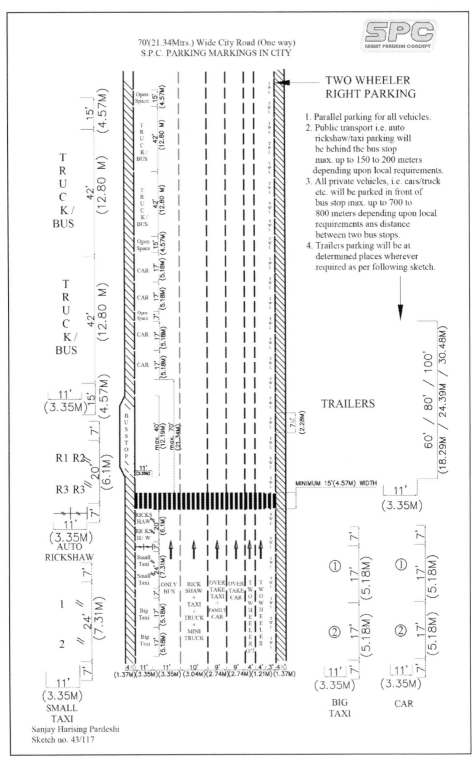

70'(21.34Mtrs.) Wide City Road (One way)
S.P.C. PARKING MARKINGS IN CITY

TWO WHEELER
RIGHT PARKING

1. Parallel parking for all vehicles.
2. Public transport i.e. auto
   rickshaw/taxi parking will
   be behind the bus stop
   max. up to 150 to 200 meters
   depending upon local requirements.
3. All private vehicles, i.e. cars/truck
   etc. will be parked in front of
   bus stop max. up to 700 to
   800 meters depending upon local
   requirements ans distance
   between two bus stops.
4. Trailers parking will be at
   determined places wherever
   required as per following sketch.

TRAILERS

MINIMUM 15'(4.57M) WIDTH

Sanjay Harising Pardeshi
Sketch no. 43/117

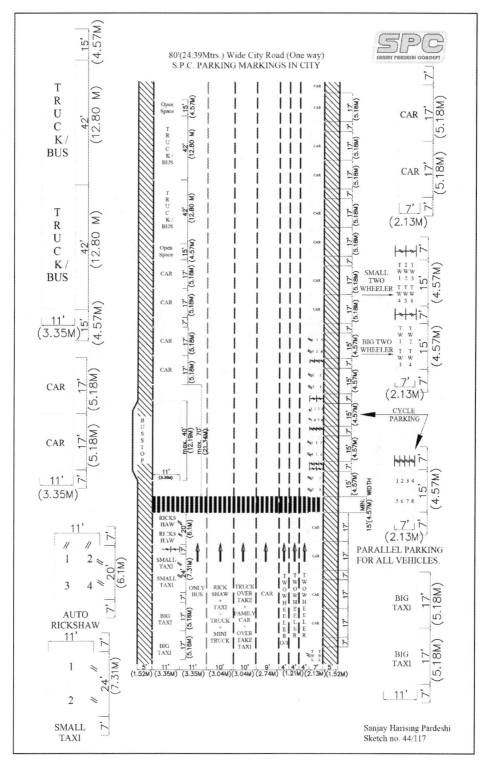

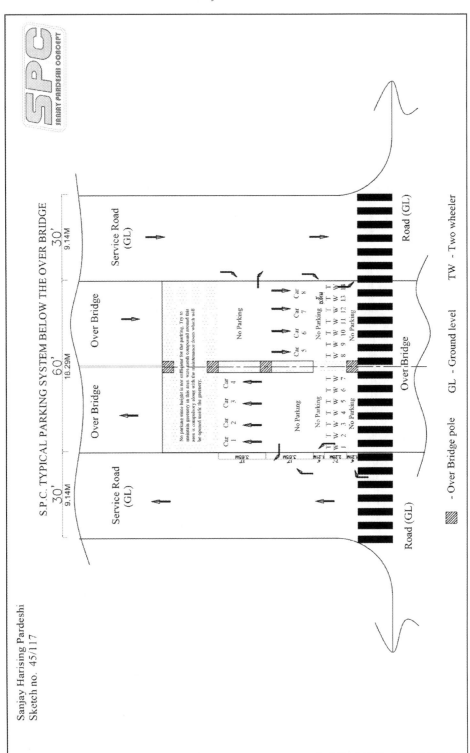

Sanjay Harising Pardeshi
Sketch no. 45/117

-Forward National clock by an hour-

If we all Indians start our work

one hour early in the morning

and finish an hour

early in the evening or at night,

crores of eletricity units will be saved !

And Load shedding will be

just another phrase in the dictionary...

something as extinct as the dinosaurs !

SANJAY PARDESHI

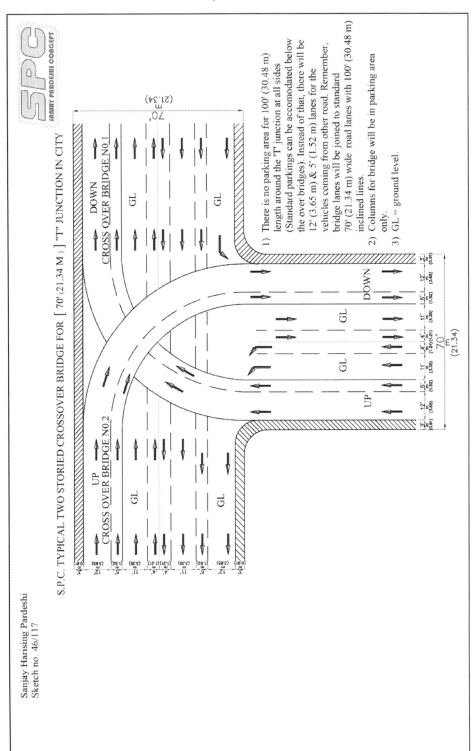

S.P.C. TYPICAL TWO STORIED CROSSOVER BRIDGE FOR [70' (21.34 M.)] "T" JUNCTION IN CITY

1) There is no parking area for 100' (30.48 m) length around the 'T' junction at all sides (Standard parkings can be accomodated below the over bridges). Instead of that, there will be 12' (3.65 m) & 5' (1.52 m) lanes for the vehicles coming from other road. Remember, bridge lanes will be joined to standard 70' (21.34 m) wide road lanes with 100' (30.48 m) inclined lines.

2) Columns for bridge will be in parking area only.

3) GL = ground level.

Sanjay Harising Pardeshi
Sketch no. 46/117

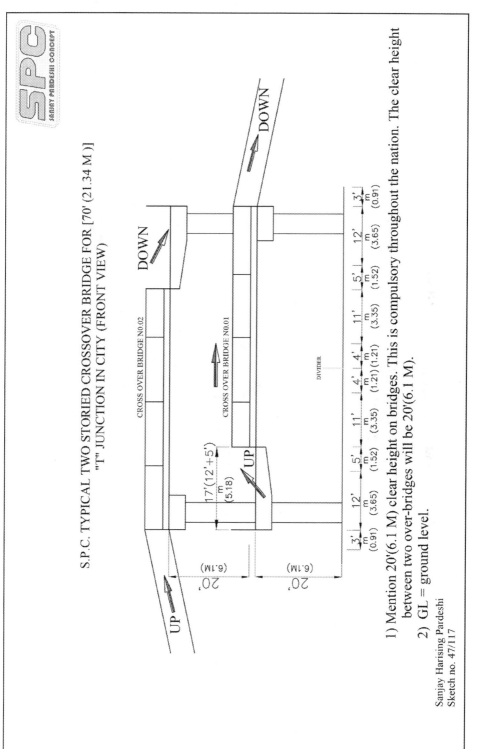

S.P.C. TYPICAL TWO STORIED CROSSOVER BRIDGE FOR [70' (21.34 M)]
"T" JUNCTION IN CITY (FRONT VIEW)

1) Mention 20'(6.1 M) clear height on bridges. This is compulsory throughout the nation. The clear height between two over-bridges will be 20'(6.1 M).

2) GL = ground level.

Sanjay Harising Pardeshi
Sketch no. 47/117

97

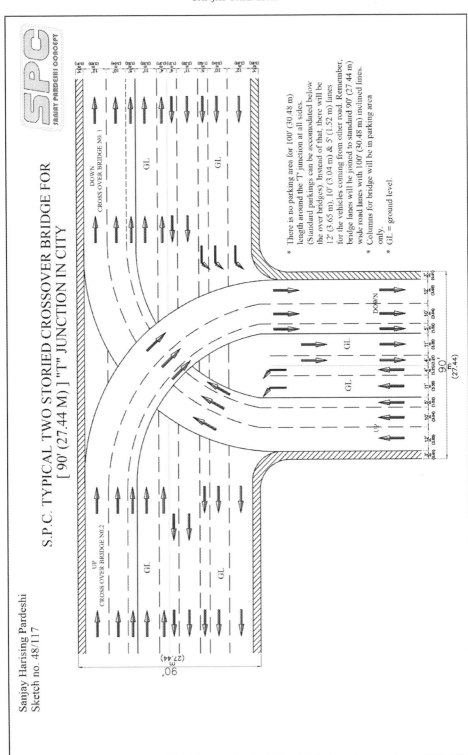

Sanjay Harising Pardeshi
Sketch no. 48/117

S.P.C. TYPICAL TWO STORIED CROSSOVER BRIDGE FOR
[90' (27.44 M)] "T" JUNCTION IN CITY

* There is no parking area for 100' (30.48 m) length around the 'T' junction at all sides. (Standard parkings can be accomodated below the over bridges). Instead of that, there will be 12' (3.65 m), 10' (3.04 m) & 5' (1.52 m) lanes for the vehicles coming from either road. Remember, bridge lanes will be joined to standard 90' (27.44 m) wide road lanes with 100' (30.48 m) inclined lines.
* Columns for bridge will be in parking area only.
* GL. = ground level.

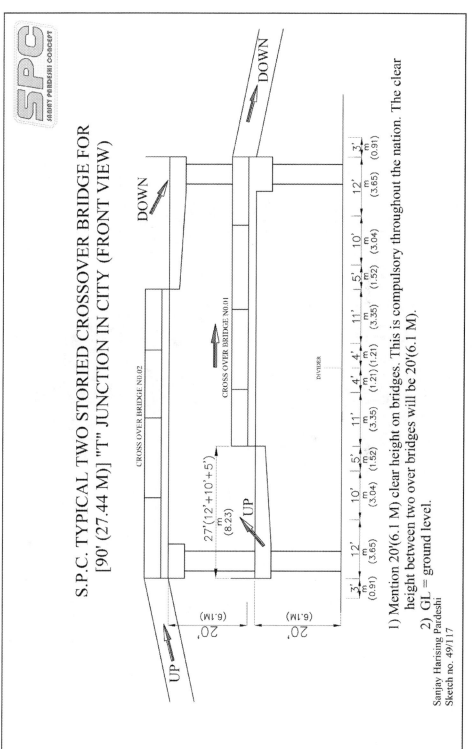

S.P.C. TYPICAL TWO STORIED CROSSOVER BRIDGE FOR [90' (27.44 M)] "T" JUNCTION IN CITY (FRONT VIEW)

1) Mention 20'(6.1 M) clear height on bridges. This is compulsory throughout the nation. The clear height between two over bridges will be 20'(6.1 M).

2) GL = ground level.

Sanjay Harising Pardeshi
Sketch no. 49/117

Sanjay Harising Pardeshi

Sketch no. 50/117   S.P.C. TYPICAL THREE STORIED CROSSOVER BRIDGE IN CITY FOR SQUARE ON 70' (21.34 M) WIDE ROAD

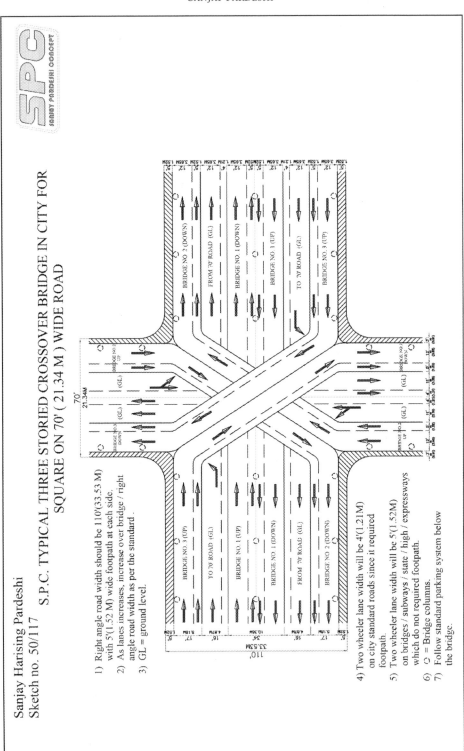

1) Right angle road width should be 110'(33.53 M) with 5'(1.52 M) wide footpath at each side.

2) As lanes increases, increase over bridge / right angle road width as per the standard .

3) GL = ground level.

4) Two wheeler lane width will be 4'(1.21M) on city standard roads since it required footpath.

5) Two wheeler lane width will be 5'(1.52M) on bridges / subways / state / high / expressways which do not required footpath.

6) ○ = Bridge columns.

7) Follow standard parking system below the bridge.

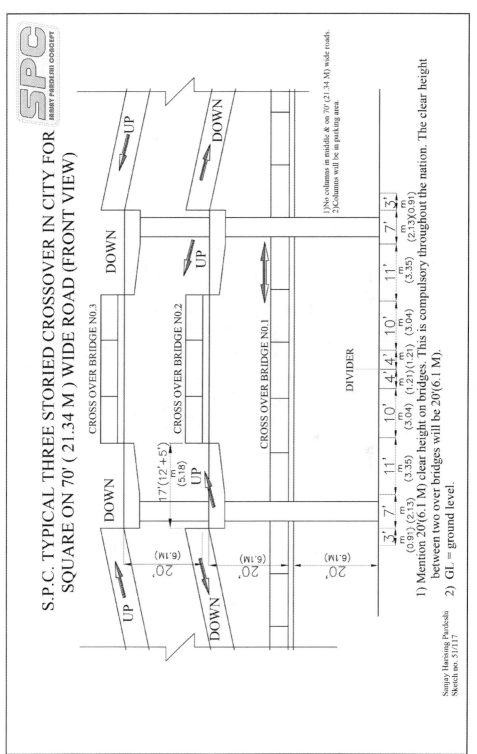

S.P.C. TYPICAL THREE STORIED CROSSOVER IN CITY FOR SQUARE ON 70' (21.34 M) WIDE ROAD (FRONT VIEW)

1) No columns in middle & on 70' (21.34 M) wide roads.
2) Columns will be in parking area.

1) Mention 20'(6.1 M) clear height on bridges. This is compulsory throughout the nation. The clear height between two over bridges will be 20'(6.1 M).
2) GL = ground level.

Sanjay Harising Pardeshi
Sketch no. 51/117

101

Sanjay Harising Pardeshi
Sketch no. 52/117

S.P.C. TYPICAL THREE STORIED CROSSOVER BRIDGE IN CITY FOR
SQUATE ON 90' (27.44M) WIDE ROAD

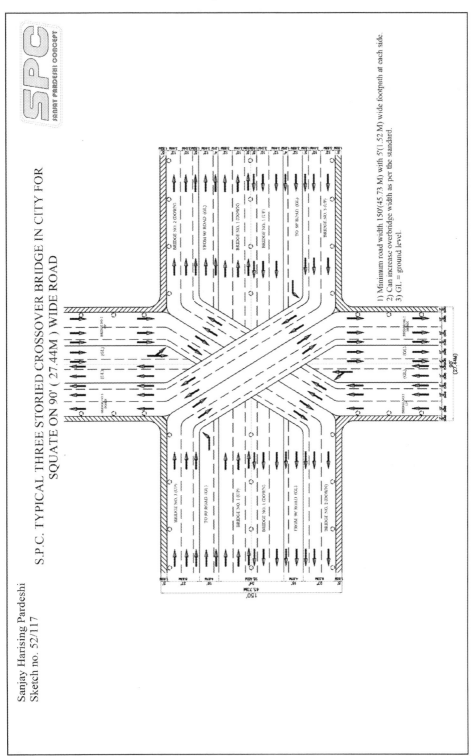

1) Minimum road width 150'(45.73 M) with 5'(1.52 M) wide footpath at each side.
2) Can increase overbridge width as per the standard.
3) GL = ground level.

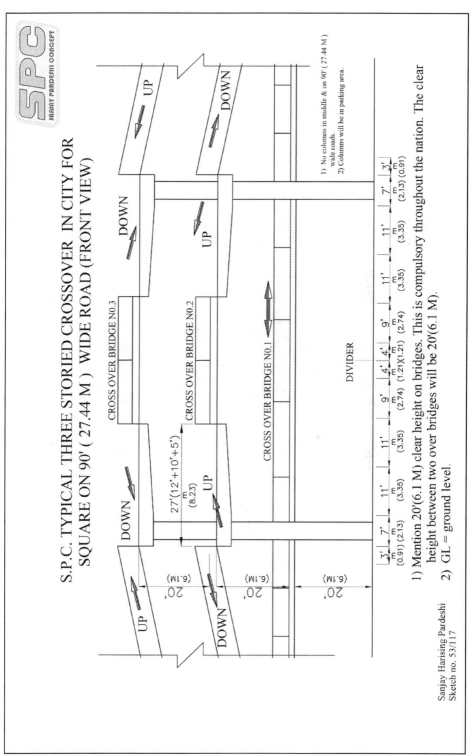

S.P.C. TYPICAL THREE STORIED CROSSOVER IN CITY FOR SQUARE ON 90' (27.44 M) WIDE ROAD (FRONT VIEW)

CROSS OVER BRIDGE N0.3

CROSS OVER BRIDGE N0.2

CROSS OVER BRIDGE N0.1

DIVIDER

27'(12'+10'+5')
m
(8.23)

UP
DOWN

1) Mention 20'(6.1 M) clear height on bridges. This is compulsory throughout the nation. The clear height between two over bridges will be 20'(6.1 M).

2) GL = ground level.

1) No columns in middle & on 90' (27.44 M) wide roads.
2) Columns will be in parking area.

Sanjay Harising Pardeshi
Sketch no. 53/117

Sanjay Harising Pardeshi
Sketch no. 54/117

S.P.C. TYPICAL THREE STORIED CROSSOVER BRIDGE IN CITY
FOR FIVE ROADS (Alternative no.1)

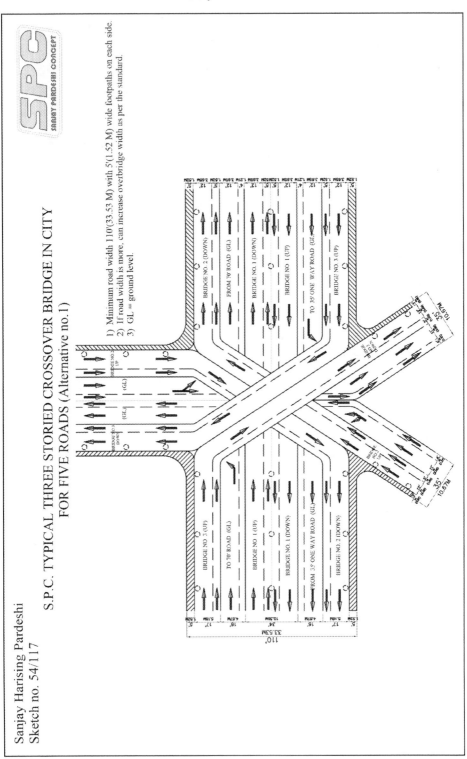

1) Minimum road width 110'(33.53 M) with 5'(1.52 M) wide footpaths on each side.
2) If road width is more, can increase overbridge width as per the standard.
3) GL = ground level.

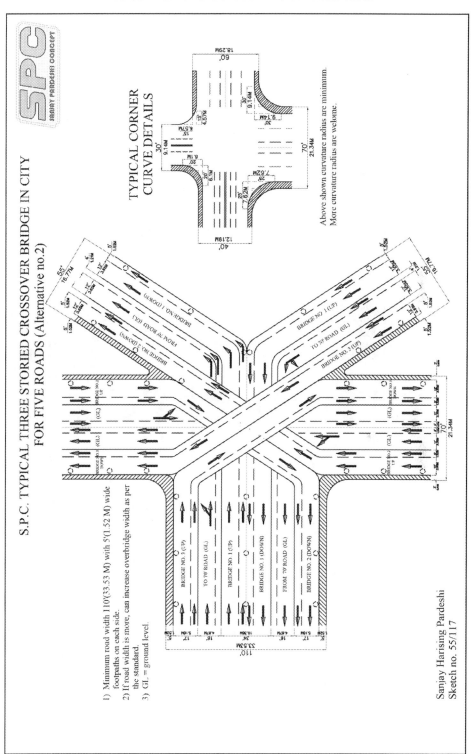

S.P.C. TYPICAL THREE STORIED CROSSOVER BRIDGE IN CITY
FOR FIVE ROADS (Alternative no.2)

TYPICAL CORNER
CURVE DETAILS

Above shown curvature radius are minimum.
More curvature radius are welcome.

1) Minimum road width 110'(33.53 M) with 5'(1.52 M) wide footpaths on each side.
2) If road width is more, can increase overbridge width as per the standard.
3) GL. = ground level.

Sanjay Harisingh Pardeshi
Sketch no. 55/117

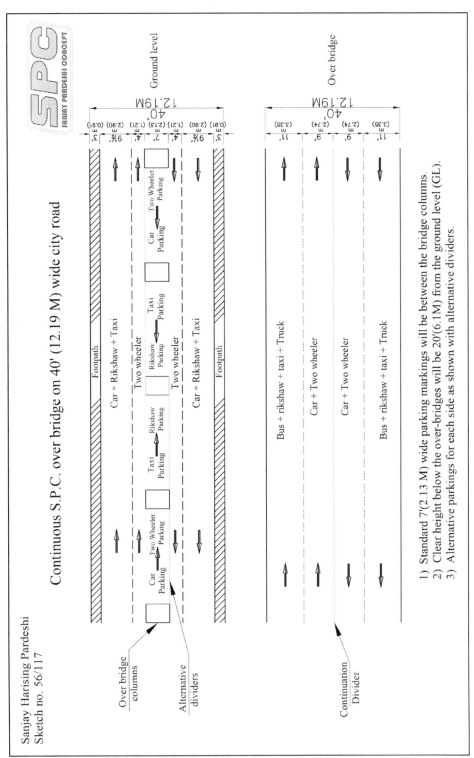

Sanjay Harising Pardeshi
Sketch no. 56/117

Continuous S.P.C. over bridge on 40' (12.19 M) wide city road

Ground level

Over bridge

1) Standard 7'(2.13 M) wide parking markings will be between the bridge columns.
2) Clear height below the over-bridges will be 20'(6.1M) from the ground level (GL).
3) Alternative parkings for each side as shown with alternative dividers.

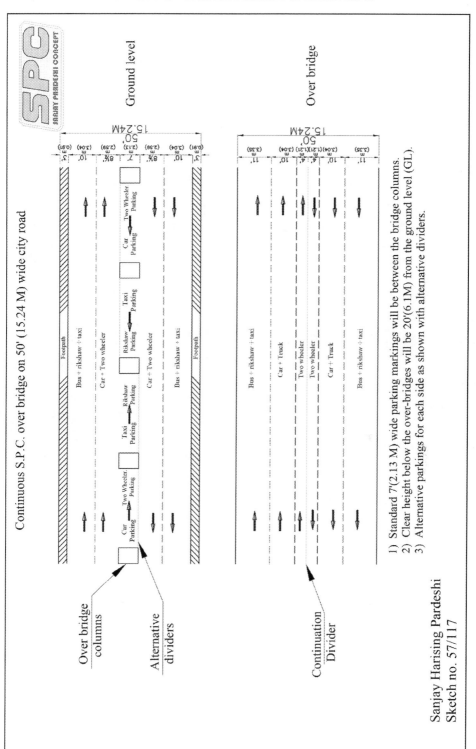

Continuous S.P.C. over bridge on 50' (15.24 M) wide city road

Ground level

Over bridge

1) Standard 7'(2.13 M) wide parking markings will be between the bridge columns.
2) Clear height below the over-bridges will be 20'(6.1M) from the ground level (GL).
3) Alternative parkings for each side as shown with alternative dividers.

Sanjay Harising Pardeshi
Sketch no. 57/117

Over bridge columns

Alternative dividers

Continuation Divider

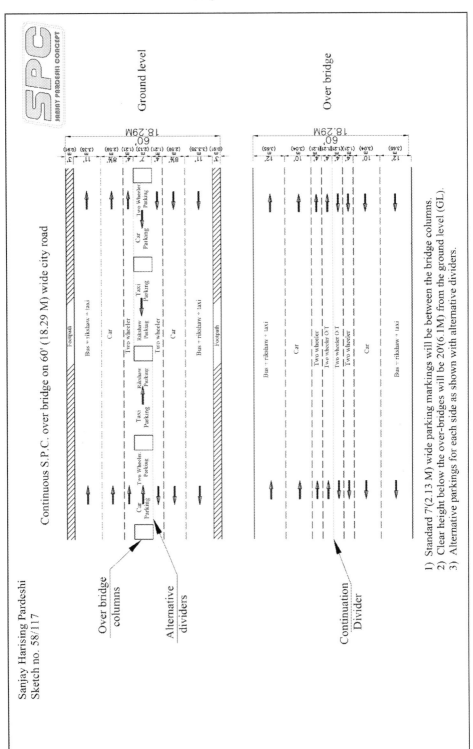

Sanjay Harising Pardeshi
Sketch no. 58/117

Continuous S.P.C. over bridge on 60' (18.29 M) wide city road

Ground level

Over bridge

Over bridge columns

Alternative dividers

Continuation Divider

1) Standard 7'(2.13 M) wide parking markings will be between the bridge columns.
2) Clear height below the over-bridges will be 20'(6.1M) from the ground level (GL).
3) Alternative parkings for each side as shown with alternative dividers.

S.P.C. TYPICAL ZEBRA CROSSING & SIGNAL SYSTEM FOR "T" JUNCTION IN CITY

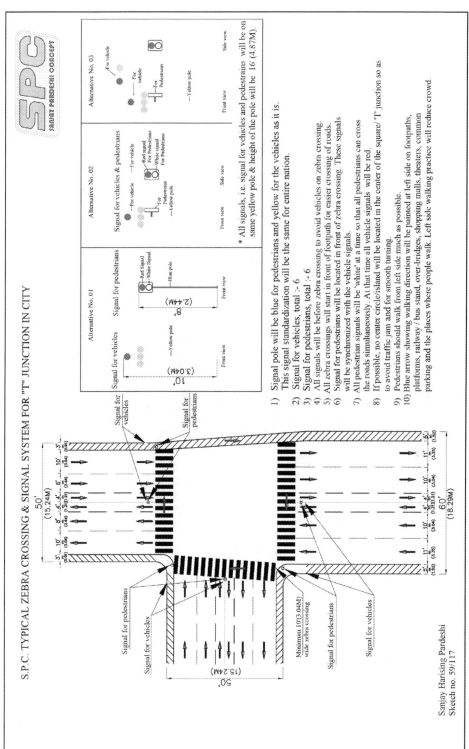

Alternative No. 01

Signal for vehicles   Signal for pedestrians

Alternative No. 02

Signal for vehicles & pedestrians

Alternative No. 03

* All signals, i.e. signal for vehicles and pedestrains will be on same yellow pole & height of the pole will be 16' (4.87M).

1) Signal pole will be blue for pedestrians and yellow for the vehicles as it is. This signal standardization will be the same for entire nation.

2) Signal for vehicles, total :- 6

3) Signal for pedestrians, total :- 6

4) All signals will be before zebra crossing to avoid vehicles on zebra crossing.

5) All zebra crossings will start in front of footpath for easier crossing of roads.

6) Signal for pedestrians will be located in front of zebra crossing. These signals will be synchronized with the vehicle signals.

7) All pedestrian signals will be 'white' at a time so that all pedestrians can cross the roads simultaneously. At that time all vehicle signals will be red.

8) If possible, no center circle/island will be located in the center of the square/ 'T' junction so as to avoid traffic jam and for smooth turning.

9) Pedestrians should walk from left side much as possible.

10) Blue arrow showing walking direction will be painted at left side on footpaths, platforms, railway / bus stand, over-bridges, shopping malls, theaters, common parking and the places where people walk. Left side walking practice will reduce crowd.

Sanjay Harising Pardeshi
Sketch no. 59/117

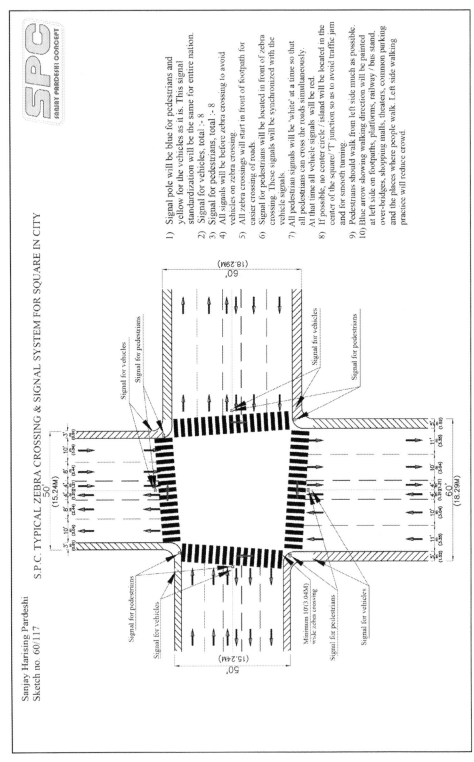

S.P.C. TYPICAL ZEBRA CROSSING & SIGNAL SYSTEM FOR SQUARE IN CITY

Sanjay Harising Pardeshi
Sketch no. 60/117

1) Signal pole will be blue for pedestrians and yellow for the vehicles as it is. This signal standardization will be the same for entire nation.

2) Signal for vehicles, total :- 8

3) Signal for pedestrians, total :- 8

4) All signals will be before zebra crossing to avoid vehicles on zebra crossing.

5) All zebra crossings will start in front of footpath for easier crossing of roads.

6) Signal for pedestrians will be located in front of zebra crossing. These signals will be synchronized with the vehicle signals.

7) All pedestrian signals will be 'white' at a time so that all pedestrians can cross the roads simultaneously. At that time all vehicle signals will be red.

8) If possible, no center circle / island will be located in the center of the square/'T' junction so as to avoid traffic jam and for smooth turning.

9) Pedestrians should walk from left side much as possible.

10) Blue arrow showing walking direction will be painted at left side on footpaths, platforms, railway / bus stand. over-bridges, shopping malls, theaters, common parking and the places where people walk. Left side walking practice will reduce crowd.

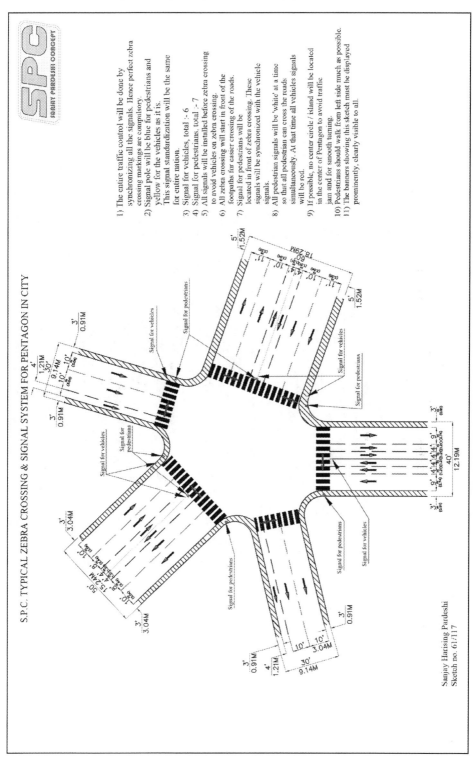

S.P.C. TYPICAL ZEBRA CROSSING & SIGNAL SYSTEM FOR PENTAGON IN CITY

1) The entire traffic control will be done by synchronizing all the signals. Hence perfect zebra crossing markings are compulsory.

2) Signal pole will be blue for pedestrians and yellow for the vehicles as it is.
   This signal standardization will be the same for entire nation.

3) Signal for vehicles, total :- 6

4) Signal for pedestrians. total :- 7

5) All signals will be installed before zebra crossing to avoid vehicles on zebra crossing.

6) All zebra crossing will start in front of the footpaths for easier crossing of the roads.

7) Signal for pedestrians will be located in front of zebra crossing. These signals will be synchronized with the vehicle signals.

8) All pedestrian signals will be 'white' at a time so that all pedestrian can cross the roads simultaneously. At that time all vehicles signals will be red.

9) If possible, no center circle / island will be located in the center of Pentagon to avoid traffic jam and for smooth turning.

10) Pedestrians should walk from left side much as possible.

11) The banners showing this sketch must be displayed prominently, clearly visible to all.

Sanjay Harising Pardeshi
Sketch no. 61/117

111

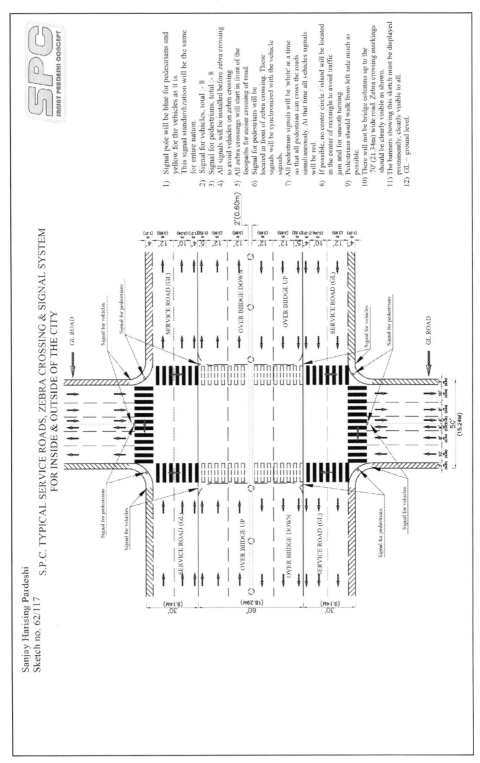

Sanjay Harising Pardeshi
Sketch no. 62/117   S.P.C. TYPICAL SERVICE ROADS, ZEBRA CROSSING & SIGNAL SYSTEM
FOR INSIDE & OUTSIDE OF THE CITY

1) Signal pole will be blue for pedestrians and yellow for the vehicles as it is. This signal standardization will be the same for entire nation.

2) Signal for vehicles, total :- 8

3) Signal for pedestrians, total :- 8

4) All signals will be installed before zebra crossing to avoid vehicles on zebra crossing

5) All zebra crossings will start in front of the footpaths for easier crossing of road

6) Signal for pedestrians will be located in front of zebra crossing. These signals will be synchronized with the vehicle signals.

7) All pedestrian signals will be 'white' at a time so that all pedestrian can cross the roads simultaneously. At that time all vehicles signals will be red.

8) If possible, no center circle / island will be located in the center of rectangle to avoid traffic jam and for smooth turning.

9) Pedestrians should walk from left side much as possible.

10) There will not be bridge columns up to the 70' (21.34m) wide road. Zebra crossing markings should be clearly visible as shown.

11) The banners showing this sketch must be displayed prominently, clearly visible to all.

12) GL - ground level.

S.P.C. INTERCITY BUS STAND & ONE WAY FRONT ROAD
(Alternative no.1)

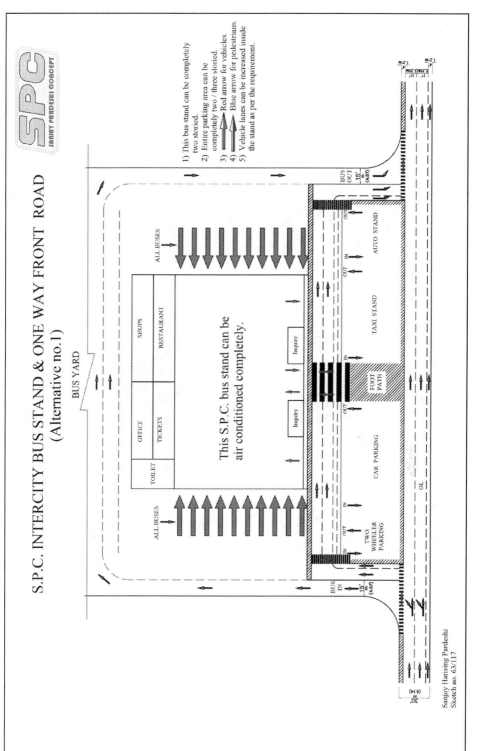

1) This bus stand can be completely two storied.
2) Entire parking area can be completely two / three storied.
3) Red arrow for vehicles.
4) Blue arrow for pedestrians.
5) Vehicle lanes can be increased inside the stand as per the requirement.

This S.P.C. bus stand can be air conditioned completely.

Sanjay Harising Pardeshi
Sketch no. 63/117

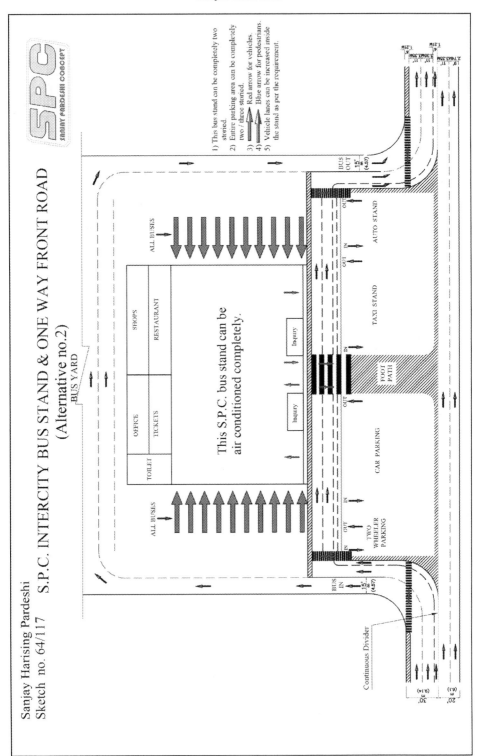

Sanjay Harising Pardeshi
Sketch no. 64/117   S.P.C. INTERCITY BUS STAND & ONE WAY FRONT ROAD
(Alternative no.2)

1) This bus stand can be completely two storied.
2) Entire parking area can be completely two / three storied.
3) Red arrow for vehicles.
4) Blue arrow for pedestrians.
5) Vehicle lanes can be increased inside the stand as per the requirement.

This S.P.C. bus stand can be air conditioned completely.

S.P.C. INTERCITY BUS STAND & TWO WAY FRONT ROAD

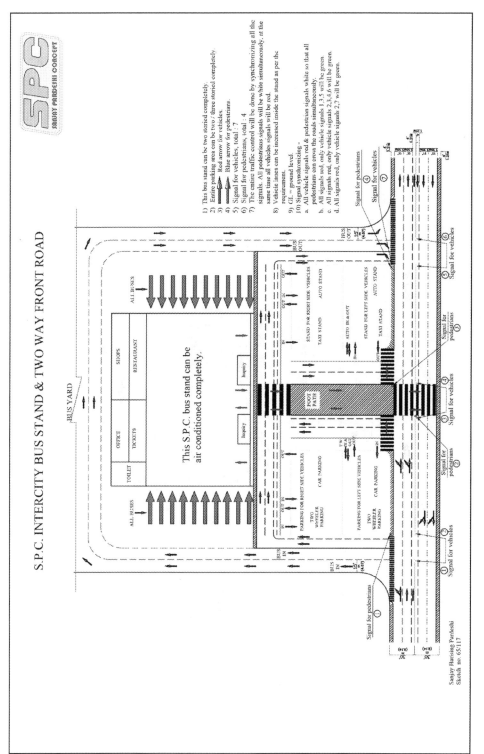

1) This bus stand can be two storied completely.
2) Entire parking area can be two / three storied completely.
3) ↑ Red arrow for vehicles.
4) ↑ Blue arrow for pedestrians.
5) Signal for vehicles, total : 7
6) Signal for pedestrians, total : 4
7) The entire traffic control will be done by synchronizing all the signals. All pedestrians signals will be white so that all signals simultaneously, at the same time all vehicles signals will be red.
8) Vehicle lanes can be increased inside the stand as per the requirement.
9) GL = ground level
10) Signal synchronizing –
   a. All vehicle signals red & pedestrian signals white so that all pedestrians can cross the roads simultaneously.
   b. All signals red, only vehicle signals 1,3,5 will be green.
   c. All signals red, only vehicle signals 2,3,4,6 will be green.
   d. All signals red, only vehicle signals 2,7 will be green.

This S.P.C. bus stand can be air conditioned completely.

Sanjay Harising Pardeshi
Sketch no: 65/117

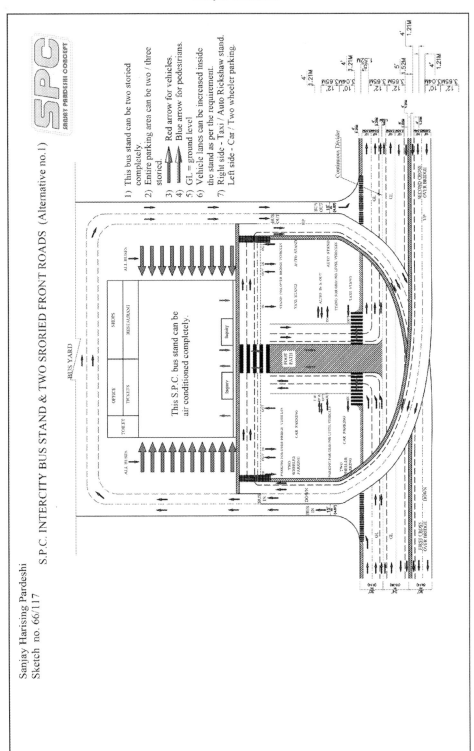

Sanjay Harising Pardeshi
Sketch no. 66/117

S.P.C. INTERCITY BUS STAND & TWO SRORIED FRONT ROADS (Alternative no.1)

1) This bus stand can be two storied completely.
2) Entire parking area can be two / three storied.
3) Red arrow for vehicles.
4) Blue arrow for pedestrians.
5) GL = ground level
6) Vehicle lanes can be increased inside the stand as per the requirement.
7) Right side - Taxi / Auto Rickshaw stand.
   Left side - Car / Two wheeler parking.

This S.P.C. bus stand can be air conditioned completely.

S.P.C. INTERCITY BUS STAND & TWO SRORIED FRONT ROADS (Alternative no.2)

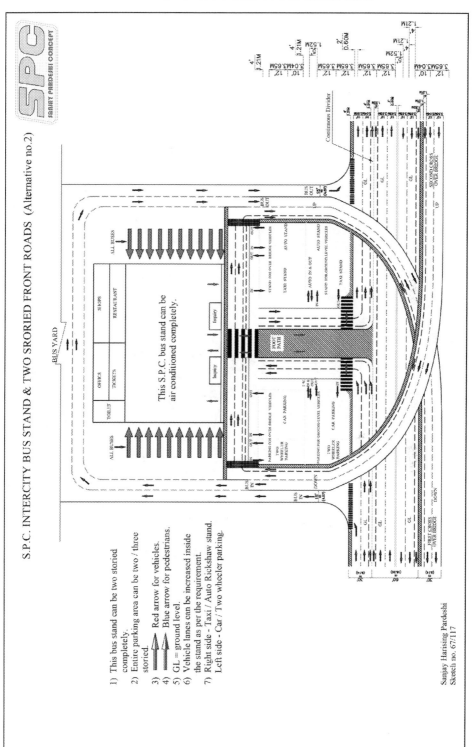

1) This bus stand can be two storied completely.
2) Entire parking area can be two / three storied.
3) ➡ Red arrow for vehicles.
4) ➡ Blue arrow for pedestrians.
5) GL = ground level.
6) Vehicle lanes can be increased inside the stand as per the requirement.
7) Right side - Taxi / Auto Rickshaw stand. Left side - Car / Two wheeler parking.

Sanjay Harising Pardeshi
Sketch no. 67/117

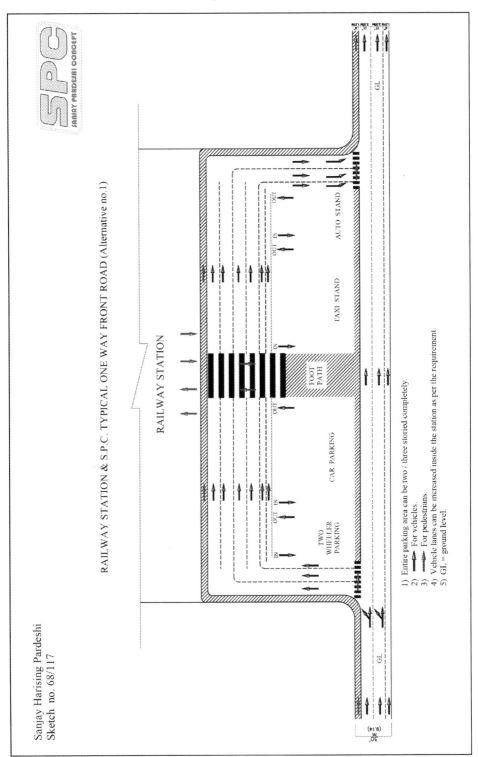

Sanjay Harising Pardeshi
Sketch no. 68/117

RAILWAY STATION & S.P.C. TYPICAL ONE WAY FRONT ROAD (Alternative no.1)

RAILWAY STATION

AUTO STAND

TAXI STAND

FOOT PATH

CAR PARKING

TWO WHEELER PARKING

1) Entire parking area can be two / three storied completely.
2) For vehicles.
3) For pedestrians.
4) Vehicle lanes can be increased inside the station as per the requirement.
5) GL = ground level.

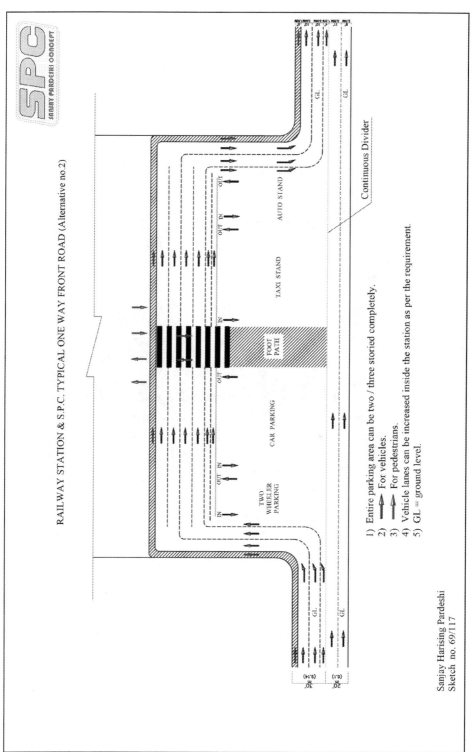

RAILWAY STATION & S.P.C. TYPICAL ONE WAY FRONT ROAD (Alternative no.2)

1) Entire parking area can be two / three storied completely.
2) → For vehicles.
3) → For pedestrians.
4) Vehicle lanes can be increased inside the station as per the requirement.
5) GL = ground level.

Sanjay Harising Pardeshi
Sketch no. 69/117

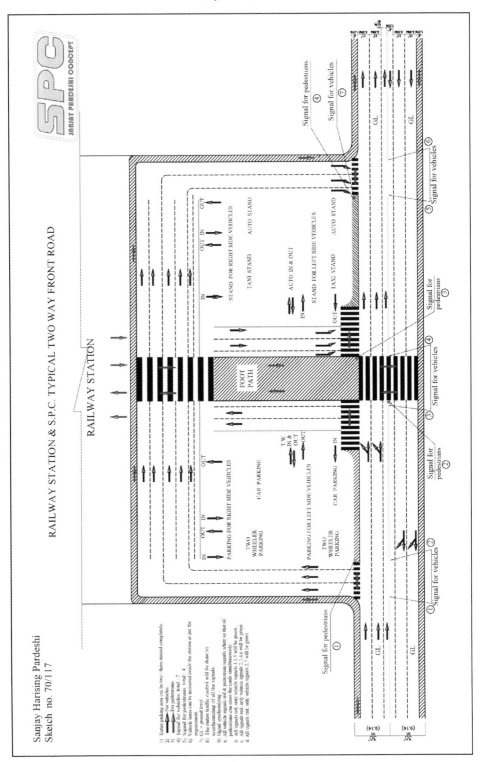

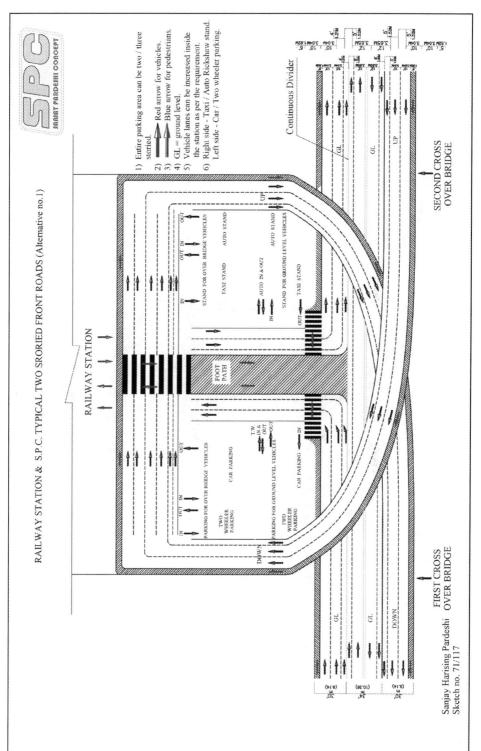

RAILWAY STATION & S.P.C. TYPICAL TWO STORIED FRONT ROADS (Alternative no.1)

1) Entire parking area can be two / three storied.
2) Red arrow for vehicles.
3) Blue arrow for pedestrians.
4) GL = ground level.
5) Vehicle lanes can be increased inside the station as per the requirement.
6) Right side - Taxi / Auto Rickshaw stand. Left side - Car / Two wheeler parking.

Continuous Divider

RAILWAY STATION

FOOT PATH

STAND FOR OVER BRIDGE VEHICLES
TAXI STAND
AUTO STAND
AUTO IN & OUT
STAND FOR GROUND LEVEL VEHICLES
AUTO STAND
TAXI STAND

PARKING FOR OVER BRIDGE VEHICLES
CAR PARKING
TWO WHEELER PARKING
PARKING FOR GROUND LEVEL VEHICLES
TWO WHEELER PARKING
CAR PARKING

SECOND CROSS OVER BRIDGE

FIRST CROSS OVER BRIDGE

Sanjay Harising Pardeshi
Sketch no. 71/117

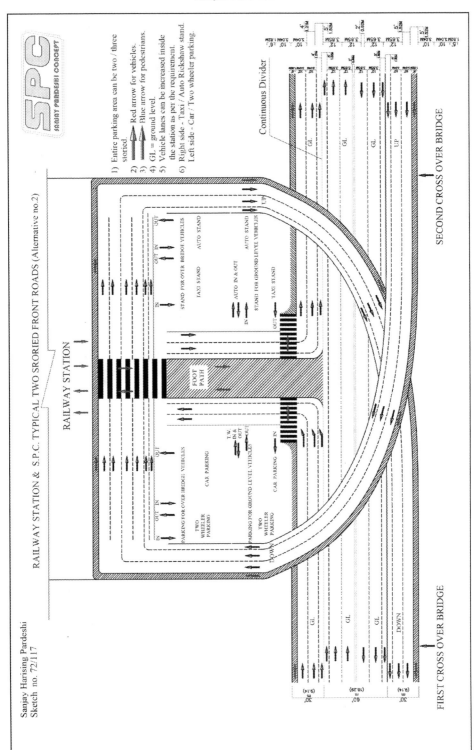

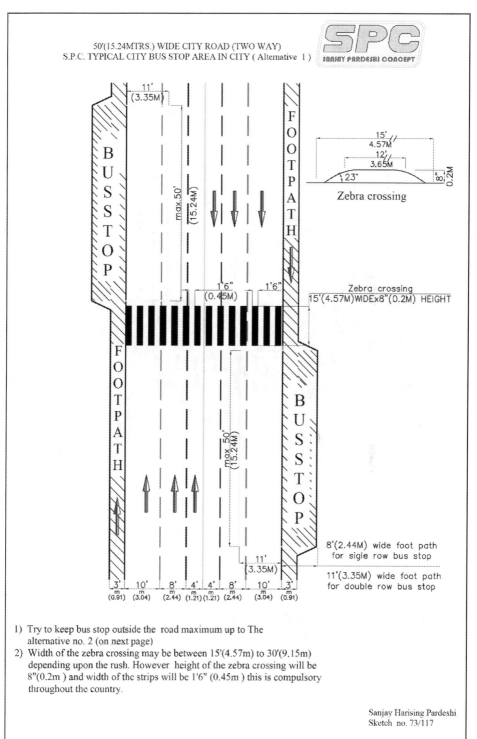

50'(15.24MTRS.) WIDE CITY ROAD (TWO WAY)
S.P.C. TYPICAL CITY BUS STOP AREA IN CITY (Alternative 1)

Zebra crossing

Zebra crossing
15'(4.57M)WIDEx8"(0.2M) HEIGHT

8'(2.44M) wide foot path
for sigle row bus stop

11'(3.35M) wide foot path
for double row bus stop

1) Try to keep bus stop outside the road maximum up to The
   alternative no. 2 (on next page)
2) Width of the zebra crossing may be between 15'(4.57m) to 30'(9.15m)
   depending upon the rush. However height of the zebra crossing will be
   8"(0.2m) and width of the strips will be 1'6" (0.45m) this is compulsory
   throughout the country.

Sanjay Harising Pardeshi
Sketch no. 73/117

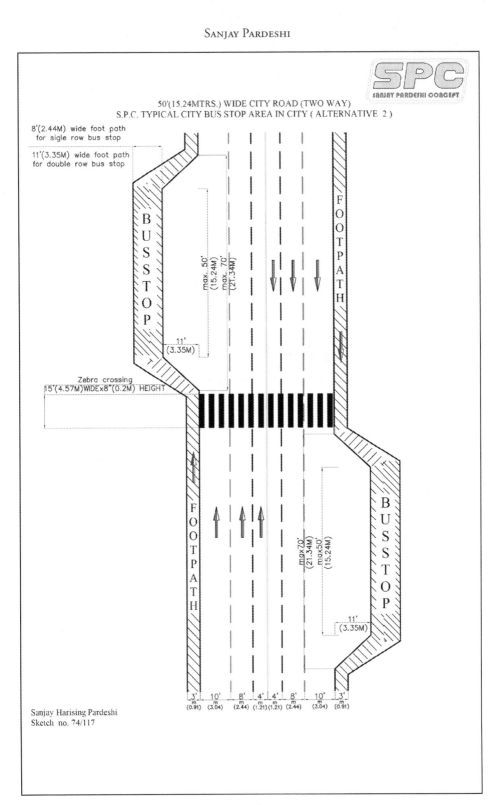

50'(15.24MTRS.) WIDE CITY ROAD (TWO WAY)
S.P.C. TYPICAL CITY BUS STOP AREA IN CITY (ALTERNATIVE 2)

8'(2.44M) wide foot path
for sigle row bus stop

11'(3.35M) wide foot path
for double row bus stop

Zebra crossing
15'(4.57M)WIDEx8"(0.2M) HEIGHT

Sanjay Harising Pardeshi
Sketch no. 74/117

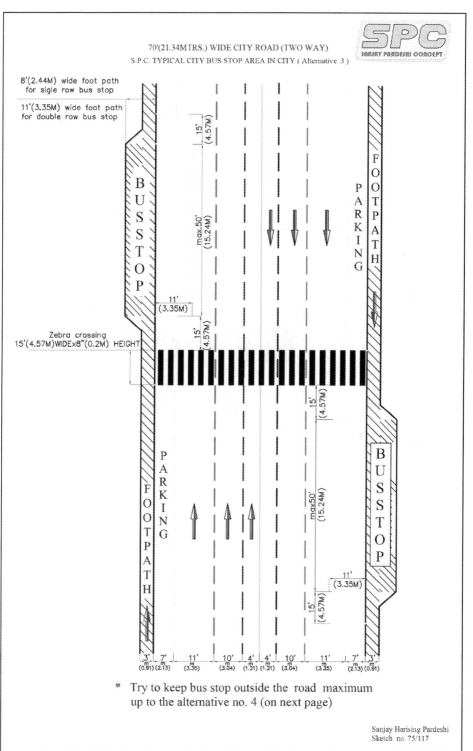

70'(21.34MTRS.) WIDE CITY ROAD (TWO WAY)

S.P.C. TYPICAL CITY BUS STOP AREA IN CITY (Alternative 3)

8'(2.44M) wide foot path for sigle row bus stop

11'(3.35M) wide foot path for double row bus stop

Zebra crossing 15'(4.57M)WIDEx8"(0.2M) HEIGHT

* Try to keep bus stop outside the road maximum up to the alternative no. 4 (on next page)

Sanjay Harising Pardeshi
Sketch no. 75/117

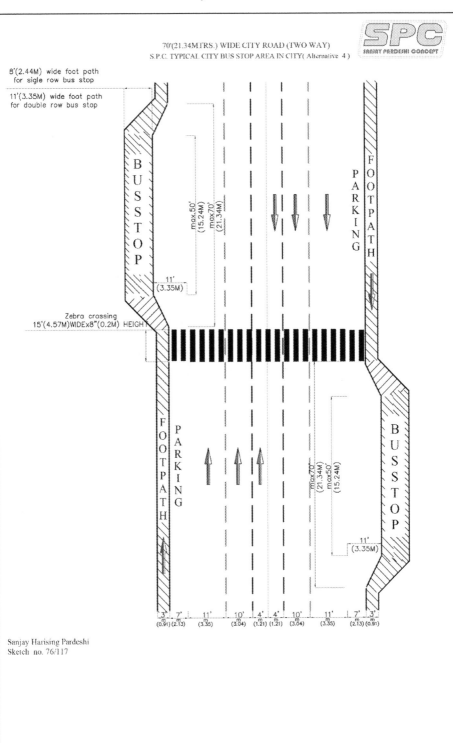

70'(21.34MTRS.) WIDE CITY ROAD (TWO WAY)
S.P.C. TYPICAL CITY BUS STOP AREA IN CITY(Alternative 4)

8'(2.44M) wide foot path
for sigle row bus stop

11'(3.35M) wide foot path
for double row bus stop

BUS STOP

PARKING

FOOTPATH

max.50'
(15.24M)

max70'
(21.34M)

11'
(3.35M)

Zebra crossing
15'(4.57M)WIDEx8"(0.2M) HEIGHT

FOOTPATH

PARKING

BUS STOP

max70'
(21.34M)

max50'
(15.24M)

11'
(3.35M)

3' 7' 11' 10' 4' 4' 10' 11' 7' 3'
(0.91)(2.13) (3.35) (3.04) (1.21)(1.21) (3.04) (3.35) (2.13)(0.91)

Sanjay Harising Pardeshi
Sketch no. 76/117

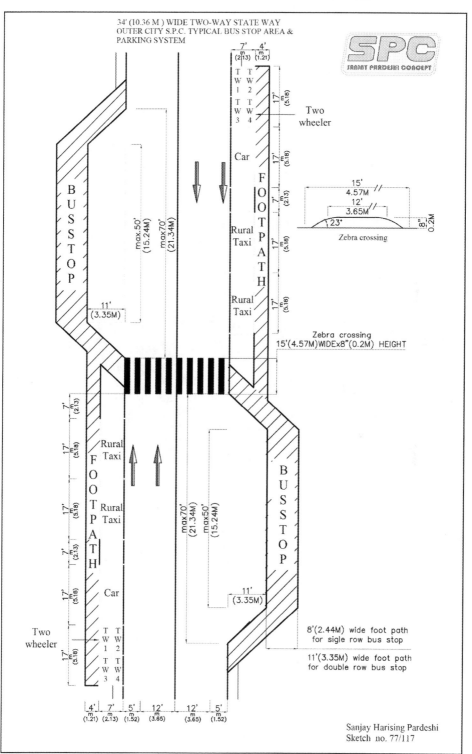

34' (10.36 M) WIDE TWO-WAY STATE WAY
OUTER CITY S.P.C. TYPICAL BUS STOP AREA &
PARKING SYSTEM

Zebra crossing
15'(4.57M)WIDEx8"(0.2M) HEIGHT

Zebra crossing

8'(2.44M) wide foot path
for sigle row bus stop

11'(3.35M) wide foot path
for double row bus stop

Sanjay Harising Pardeshi
Sketch no. 77/117

127

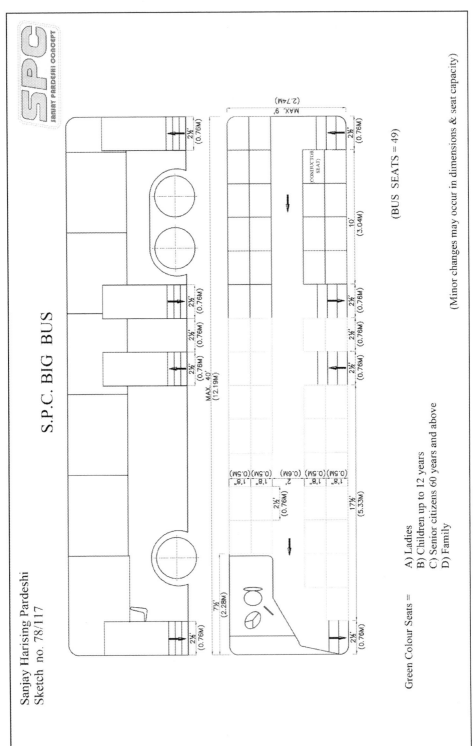

Sanjay Harising Pardeshi
Sketch no. 78/117

S.P.C. BIG BUS

CONDUCTOR SEAT

(BUS SEATS = 49)

(Minor changes may occur in dimensions & seat capacity)

Green Colour Seats =
A) Ladies
B) Children up to 12 years
C) Senior citizens 60 years and above
D) Family

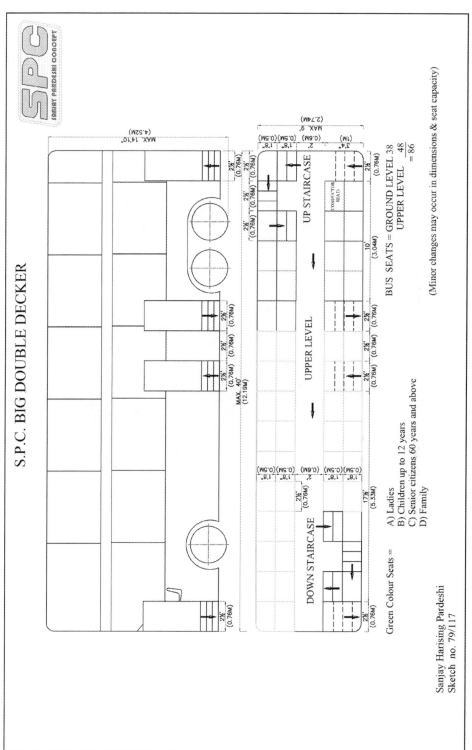

S.P.C. BIG DOUBLE DECKER

MAX. 14'10" (4.52M)

MAX. 40' (12.19M)

MAX. 9' (2.74M)

UP STAIRCASE

UPPER LEVEL

DOWN STAIRCASE

CONDUCTOR SEAT

BUS SEATS = GROUND LEVEL 38
UPPER LEVEL 48
= 86

(Minor changes may occur in dimensions & seat capacity)

Green Colour Seats =

A) Ladies
B) Children up to 12 years
C) Senior citizens 60 years and above
D) Family

Sanjay Harising Pardeshi
Sketch no. 79/117

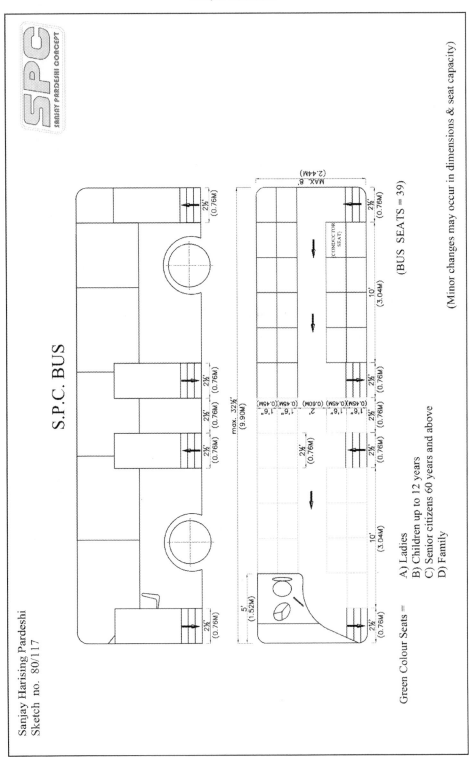

S.P.C. BUS

Sanjay Harising Pardeshi
Sketch no. 80/117

(BUS SEATS = 39)

Green Colour Seats =

A) Ladies
B) Children up to 12 years
C) Senior citizens 60 years and above
D) Family

(Minor changes may occur in dimensions & seat capacity)

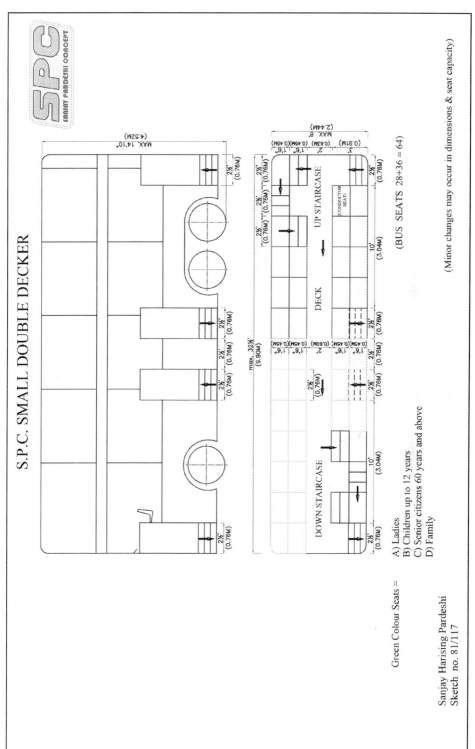

S.P.C. SMALL DOUBLE DECKER

MAX. 14'10" (4.52M)

max. 32½' (9.90M)

DOWN STAIRCASE

UP STAIRCASE

DECK

CONDUCTOR SEATS

MAX. 8' (2.44M)

(BUS SEATS 28+36 = 64)

(Minor changes may occur in dimensions & seat capacity)

Green Colour Seats =

A) Ladies
B) Children up to 12 years
C) Senior citizens 60 years and above
D) Family

Sanjay Harising Pardeshi
Sketch no. 81/117

131

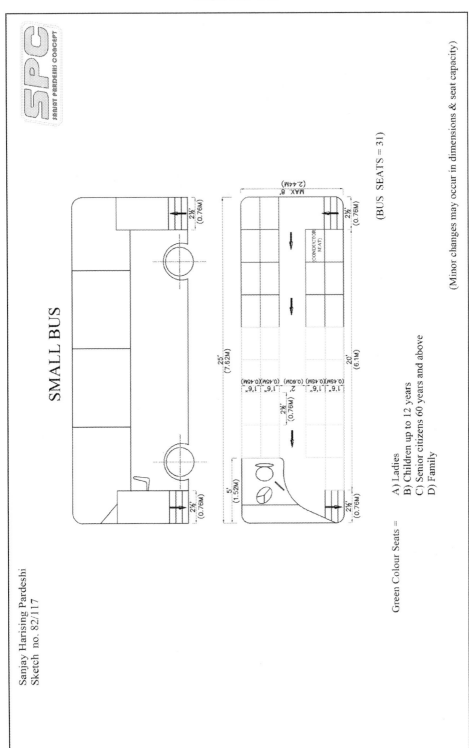

SMALL BUS

Sanjay Harising Pardeshi
Sketch no. 82/117

(BUS SEATS = 31)

(Minor changes may occur in dimensions & seat capacity)

Green Colour Seats =   A) Ladies
B) Children up to 12 years
C) Senior citizens 60 years and above
D) Family

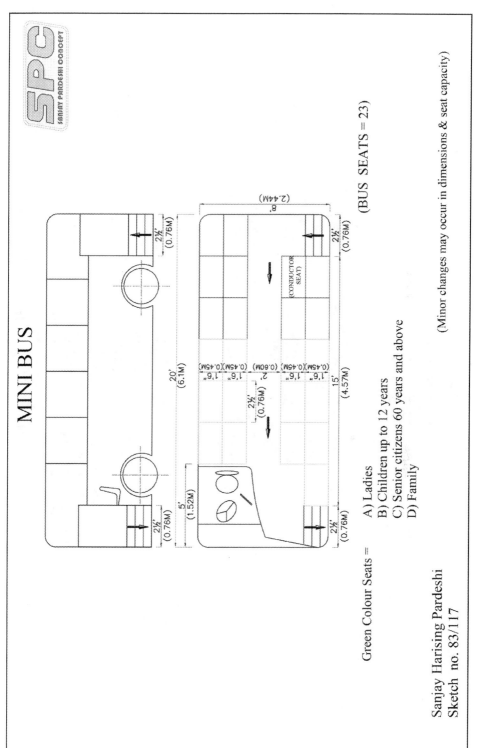

MINI BUS

SPC
SANJAY PARDESHI CONCEPT

(BUS SEATS = 23)

Green Colour Seats =

A) Ladies
B) Children up to 12 years
C) Senior citizens 60 years and above
D) Family

(Minor changes may occur in dimensions & seat capacity)

Sanjay Harising Pardeshi
Sketch no. 83/117

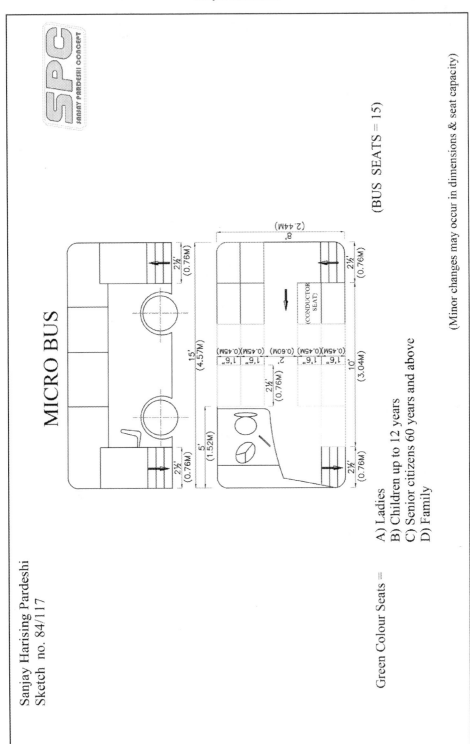

MICRO BUS

Sanjay Harising Pardeshi
Sketch no. 84/117

Green Colour Seats =

A) Ladies
B) Children up to 12 years
C) Senior citizens 60 years and above
D) Family

(BUS SEATS = 15)

(Minor changes may occur in dimensions & seat capacity)

- Only an hour for the nation -

While looking after our daily work routine,
if we all Indians do an hour's work for the nation daily,
India will develop TOTALLY in all segments
within the next 15/20 years.

For this, if all TV / radio channels come together and
fix one time slot to start the program **'AN HOUR FOR
THE NATION',** it will be a very unique step towards
the comprehensive development of India. Needless
to add that this program will be run by people
showcasing their problems (local to national),
solutions, practical projects, role models, suggestions,
information, etc. To add even more value, people
will share their positive experinces, inspiring ideas
and positive results of the changes happening in
the country. Naturally TV / radio team will be always
with them. For the last so many years, we all have
seen and heard entertainment programs. However
this **'ONE HOUR'** program can be our mainstay
for the nation's bright future.

SANJAY PARDESHI

S.P.C. CITY BUS STOP POLES FOR ALL BUSES

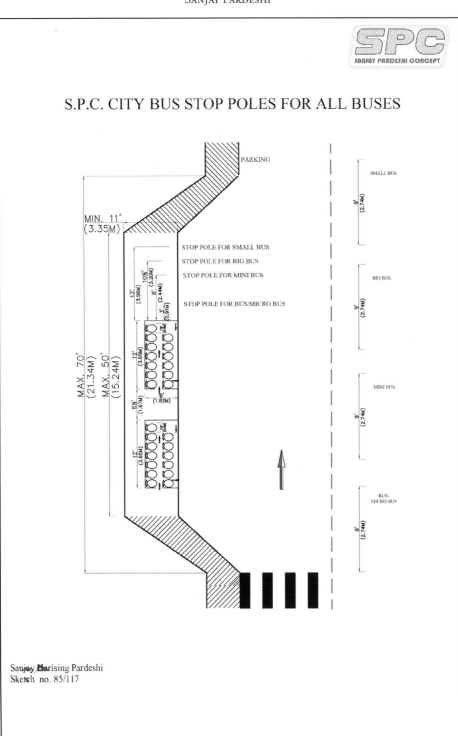

Sanjay Harising Pardeshi
Sketch no. 85/117

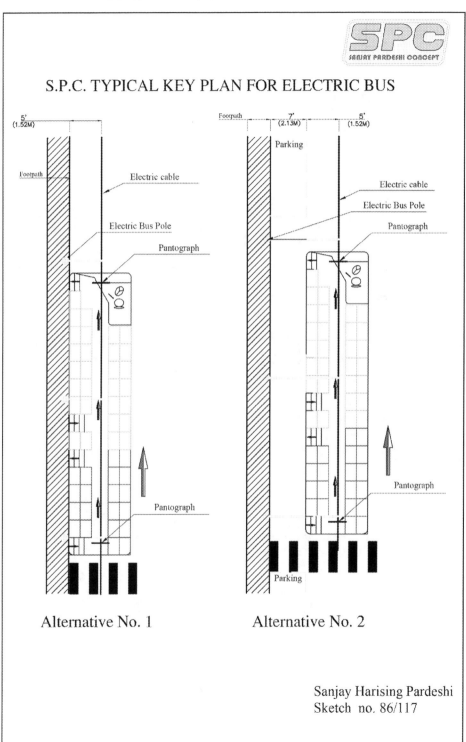

S.P.C. TYPICAL KEY PLAN FOR ELECTRIC BUS

Alternative No. 1

Alternative No. 2

Sanjay Harising Pardeshi
Sketch no. 86/117

S.P.C. BUS STOP DETAILING (ALTERNATIVE NO.1)

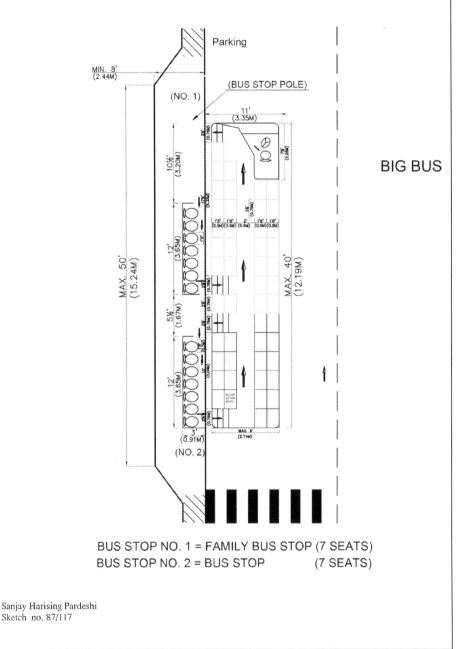

BIG BUS

BUS STOP NO. 1 = FAMILY BUS STOP (7 SEATS)
BUS STOP NO. 2 = BUS STOP (7 SEATS)

Sanjay Harising Pardeshi
Sketch no. 87/117

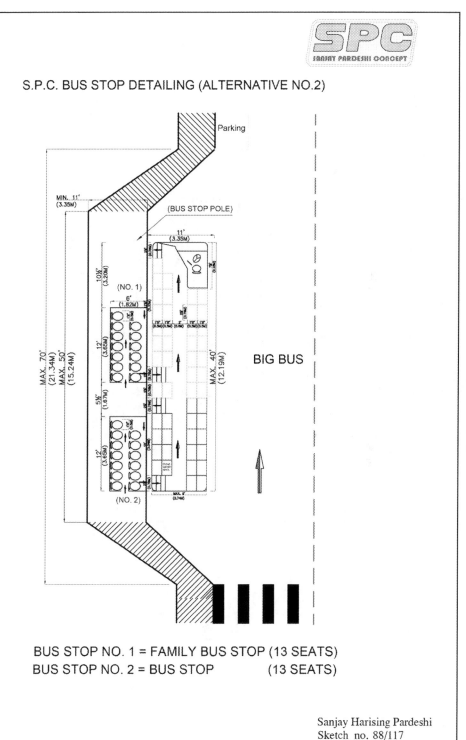

S.P.C. BUS STOP DETAILING (ALTERNATIVE NO.2)

Parking

MIN. 11'
(3.35M)

(BUS STOP POLE)

11'
(3.35M)

(NO. 1)

6'
(1.82M)

BIG BUS

(NO. 2)

BUS STOP NO. 1 = FAMILY BUS STOP (13 SEATS)
BUS STOP NO. 2 = BUS STOP (13 SEATS)

Sanjay Harising Pardeshi
Sketch no. 88/117

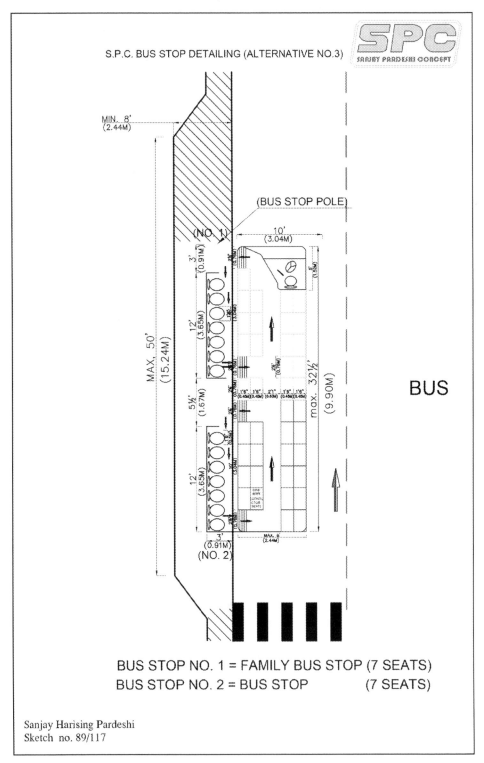

BUS STOP NO. 1 = FAMILY BUS STOP (7 SEATS)
BUS STOP NO. 2 = BUS STOP   (7 SEATS)

Sanjay Harising Pardeshi
Sketch no. 89/117

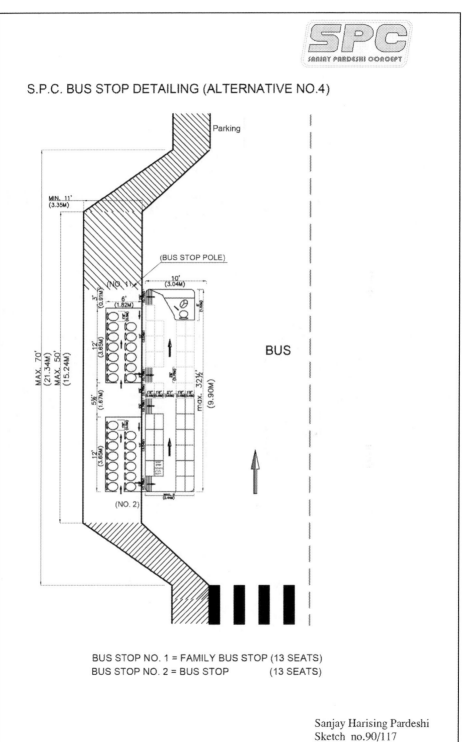

S.P.C. BUS STOP DETAILING (ALTERNATIVE NO.4)

BUS STOP NO. 1 = FAMILY BUS STOP (13 SEATS)
BUS STOP NO. 2 = BUS STOP   (13 SEATS)

Sanjay Harising Pardeshi
Sketch no.90/117

S.P.C. BUS STOP DETAILING (ALTERNATIVE NO.5)

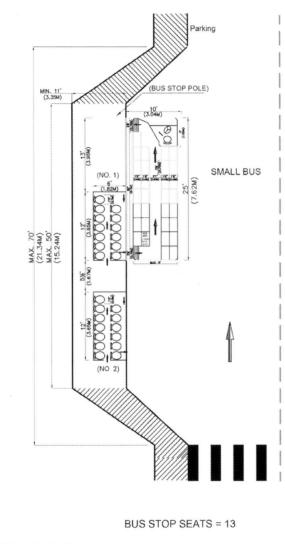

BUS STOP SEATS = 13

Sanjay Harising Pardeshi
Sketch no. 91/117

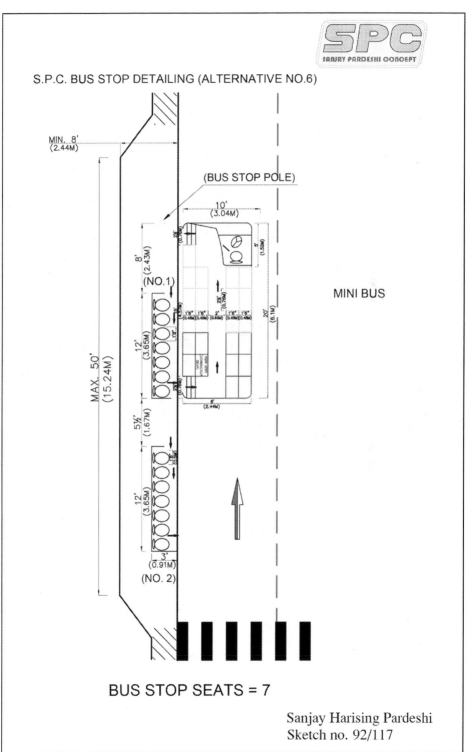

S.P.C. BUS STOP DETAILING (ALTERNATIVE NO.6)

(BUS STOP POLE)

MINI BUS

BUS STOP SEATS = 7

Sanjay Harising Pardeshi
Sketch no. 92/117

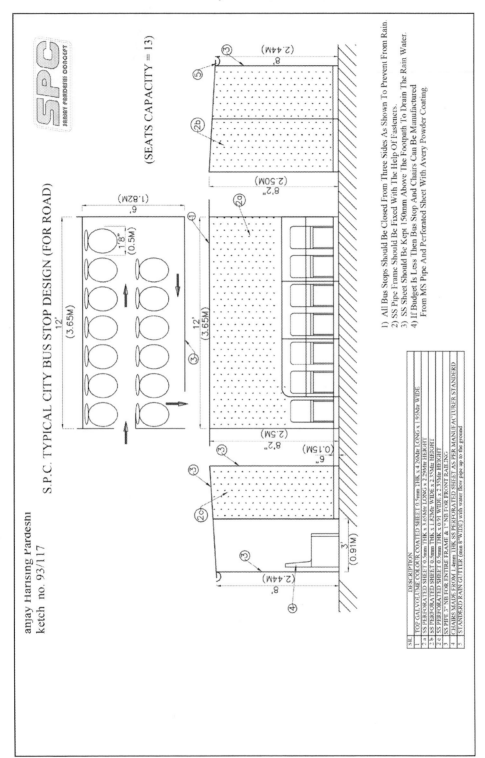

anjay Harising Pardeshi
ketch no. 93/117

S.P.C. TYPICAL CITY BUS STOP DESIGN (FOR ROAD)

(SEATS CAPACITY = 13)

1) All Bus Stops Should Be Closed From Three Sides As Shown To Prevent From Rain.
2) SS Pipe Frame Should Be Fixed With The Help Of Fasteners.
3) SS Sheet Should Be Kept 150mm Above The Footpath To Drain The Rain Water.
4) If Budget Is Less Then Bus Stop And Chairs Can Be Manufactured From MS Pipe And Perforated Sheet With Avery Powder Coating

SR	DESCRIPTION
1	TOP GALVOLUME COLOUR COATED SHEET 0.5mm THK x 4.26Mtr LONG x 1.95Mtr WIDE
2 a	SS PERFORATED SHEET 0.5mm THK x 3.65Mtr LONG x 2.29Mtr HEIGHT
2 b	SS PERFORATED SHEET 0.5mm THK x 1.82Mtr WIDE x 2.53Mtr HEIGHT
2 c	SS PERFORATED SHEET 0.5mm THK x 0.91 WIDE x 2.35Mtr HEIGHT
3	SS PIPE 3" NB FOR ENTIRE FRAME & 1" NB FOR FRONT RAILING
4	CHAIRS MADE FROM 1.4mm THK SS PERFORATED SHEET AS PER MANUFACTURER STANDERD
5	STANDERD RAIN GUTTER (min 8"WIDE) with water flow pipe up to the ground

144

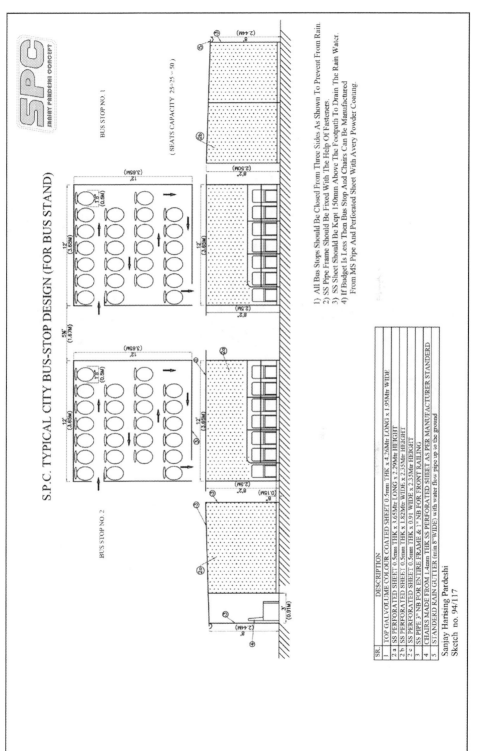

S.P.C. TYPICAL CITY BUS-STOP DESIGN (FOR BUS STAND)

BUS STOP NO. 1

(SEATS CAPACITY 25÷25 = 50)

BUS STOP NO. 2

1) All Bus Stops Should Be Closed From Three Sides As Shown To Prevent From Rain.
2) SS Pipe Frame Should Be Fixed With The Help Of Fasteners.
3) SS Sheet Should Be Kept 150mm Above The Footpath To Drain The Rain Water.
4) If Budget Is Less Then Bus Stop And Chairs Can Be Manufactured
   From MS Pipe And Perforated Sheet With Avery Powder Coating.

SR.	DESCRIPTION
1	TOP GALVOLUME COLOUR COATED SHEET 0.5mm THK x 4.26Mtr LONG x 1.95Mtr WIDE
2 a	SS PERFORATED SHEET 0.5mm THK x 3.65Mtr LONG x 2.29Mtr HEIGHT
2 b	SS PERFORATED SHEET 0.5mm THK x 1.82Mtr WIDE x 2.35Mtr HEIGHT
2 c	SS PERFORATED SHEET 0.5mm THK x 0.91 WIDE x 2.35Mtr HEIGHT
3	SS PIPE 3" NB FOR ENTIRE FRAME & 1" NB FOR FRONT RAILING
4	CHAIRS MADE FROM 1.4mm THK SS PERFORATED SHEET AS PER MANUFACTURER STANDERD
5	STANDERD RAIN GUTTER (min 8"WIDE) with water flow pipe up to the ground

Sanjay Harising Pardeshi
Sketch no. 94/117

145

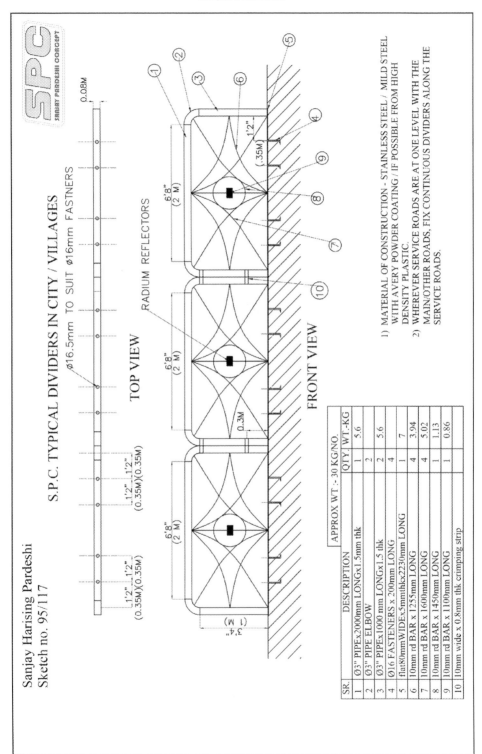

Sanjay Harising Pardeshi
Sketch no. 95/117

S.P.C. TYPICAL DIVIDERS IN CITY / VILLAGES

Ø16.5mm TO SUIT Ø16mm FASTNERS

TOP VIEW

RADIUM REFLECTORS

FRONT VIEW

SR.	DESCRIPTION	QTY.	WT.-KG
	APPROX WT :- 30 KG/NO.		
1	Ø3" PIPEx2000mm LONGx1.5mm thk	1	5.6
2	Ø3" PIPE ELBOW	2	
3	Ø3" PIPEx1000 mm LONGx1.5 thk	2	5.6
4	Ø16 FASTENERS x 200mm LONG	4	
5	flat80mmWIDEx5mmthkx2230mm LONG	1	7
6	10mm rd BAR x 1255mm LONG	4	3.94
7	10mm rd BAR x 1600mm LONG	4	5.02
8	10mm rd BAR x 1450mm LONG	1	1.13
9	10mm rd BAR x 1100mm LONG	1	0.86
10	10mm wide x 0.8mm thk crimping strip		

1) MATERIAL OF CONSTRUCTION - STAINLESS STEEL / MILD STEEL WITH A VERY POWDER COATING / IF POSSIBLE FROM HIGH DENSITY PLASTIC.

2) WHEREVER SERVICE ROADS ARE AT ONE LEVEL WITH THE MAIN/OTHER ROADS, FIX CONTINUOUS DIVIDERS ALONG THE SERVICE ROADS.

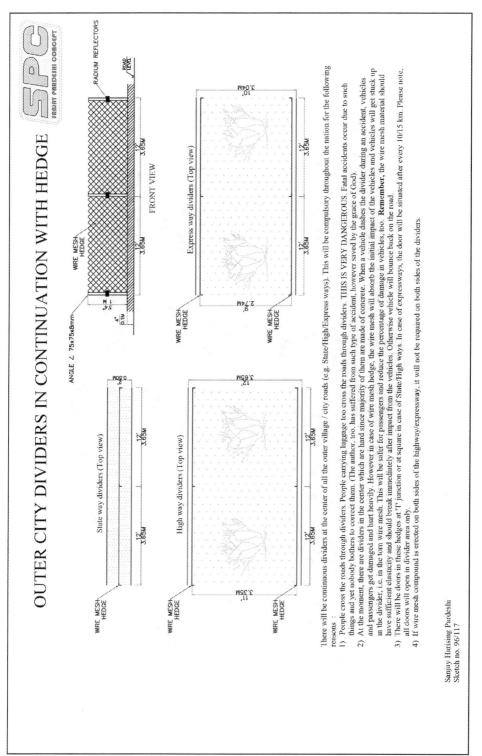

OUTER CITY DIVIDERS IN CONTINUATION WITH HEDGE

There will be continuous dividers at the center of all the outer village / city roads (e.g. State/High/Express ways). This will be compulsory throughout the nation for the following reasons :

1) People cross the roads through dividers. People carrying luggage too cross the roads through dividers. THIS IS VERY DANGEROUS. Fatal accidents occur due to such things and yet nobody bothers to correct them. (The author, too, has suffered from such type of accident, however saved by the grace of God).

2) At the moment, there are dividers in the center which are hard since majority of them are made of concrete. When a vehicle dashes the divider during an accident, vehicles and passengers get damaged and hurt heavily. However in case of wire mesh hedge, the wire mesh will absorb the initial impact of the vehicles and vehicles will get stuck up in the divider, i.e. in the torn wire mesh. This will be safer for passengers and reduce the percentage of damage in vehicles, too. **Remember**, the wire mesh material should have sufficient elasticity and should break immediately after impact from the vehicles. Otherwise vehicle will bounce back on the road.

3) There will be doors in these hedges at 'T' junction or at square in case of State/High ways. In case of expressways, the door will be situated after every 10/15 km. Please note, all doors will open in divider area only.

4) If wire mesh compound is erected on both sides of the highway/expressway, it will not be required on both sides of the dividers.

Sanjay Harising Pardeshi
Sketch no. 96/117

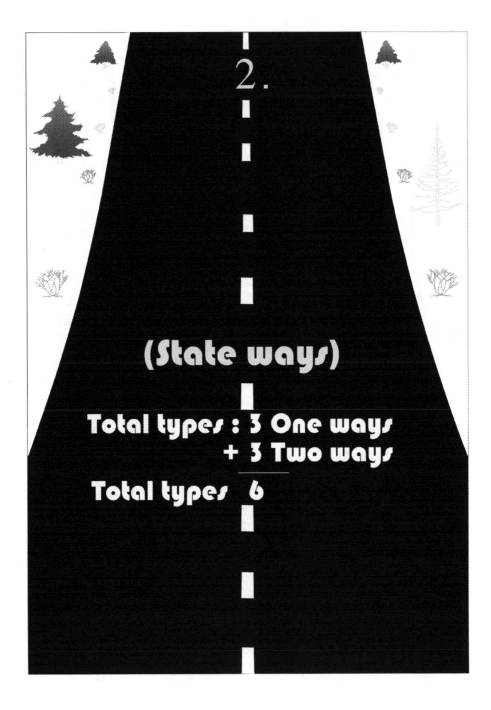

2.

(State ways)

Total types : 3 One ways
+ 3 Two ways

Total types   6

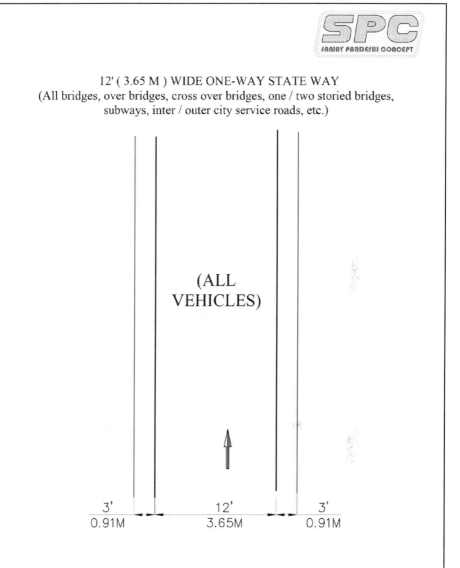

12' (3.65 M) WIDE ONE-WAY STATE WAY
(All bridges, over bridges, cross over bridges, one / two storied bridges,
subways, inter / outer city service roads, etc.)

(ALL
VEHICLES)

| 3' | 12' | 3' |
| 0.91M | 3.65M | 0.91M |

1) Every road should be kept 3'(0.91M) wider on both sides
   than its standard width for security purpose.
2) One-way approach road to connect State-way / Highway / Expressway.
3) Side margin is not required for over Bridges, cross over bridges,
   flyovers or subways.
   (However if there is enough space, then side margin can be kept).

Sanjay Harising Pardeshi
Sketch no. 97/117

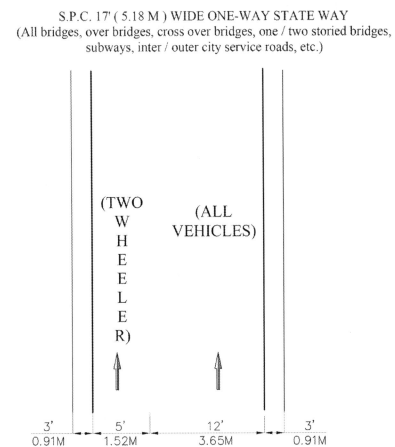

S.P.C. 17' (5.18 M) WIDE ONE-WAY STATE WAY
(All bridges, over bridges, cross over bridges, one / two storied bridges,
subways, inter / outer city service roads, etc.)

1) Every road should be kept 3'(0.91M) wider on both sides
   than its standard width for security purpose.
2) One-way approach road to connect State-way / Highway / Expressway.
3) Side margin is not required for over Bridges, cross over bridges,
   flyovers or subways.
   (However if there is enough space, then side margin can be kept).

Sanjay Harising Pardeshi
Sketch no. 98/117

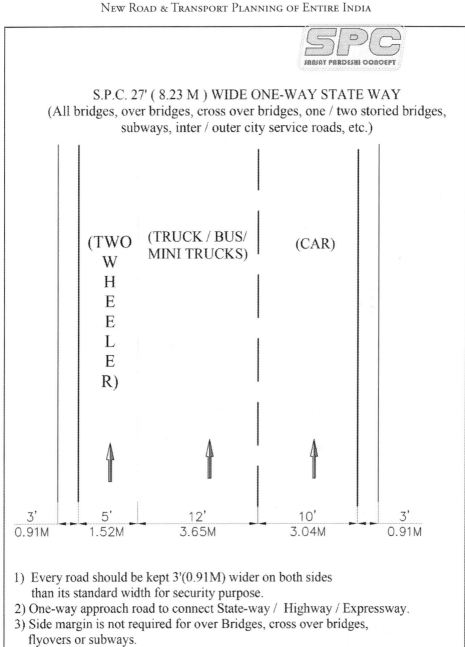

S.P.C. 27' (8.23 M) WIDE ONE-WAY STATE WAY
(All bridges, over bridges, cross over bridges, one / two storied bridges, subways, inter / outer city service roads, etc.)

(TWO WHEELER)　(TRUCK / BUS/ MINI TRUCKS)　(CAR)

| 3' | 5' | 12' | 10' | 3' |
| 0.91M | 1.52M | 3.65M | 3.04M | 0.91M |

1) Every road should be kept 3'(0.91M) wider on both sides than its standard width for security purpose.
2) One-way approach road to connect State-way / Highway / Expressway.
3) Side margin is not required for over Bridges, cross over bridges, flyovers or subways.
   (However if there is enough space, then side margin can be kept).

Sanjay Harising Pardeshi
Sketch no. 99/117

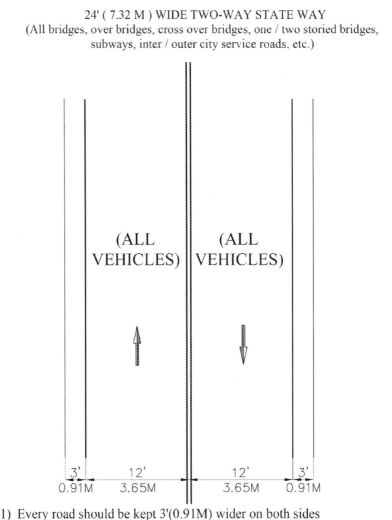

24' (7.32 M) WIDE TWO-WAY STATE WAY
(All bridges, over bridges, cross over bridges, one / two storied bridges,
subways, inter / outer city service roads, etc.)

(ALL VEHICLES) (ALL VEHICLES)

| 3' | 12' | | 12' | 3' |
| 0.91M | 3.65M | | 3.65M | 0.91M |

1) Every road should be kept 3'(0.91M) wider on both sides
   than its standard width for security purpose.
2) One-way approach road to connect State-way / Highway / Expressway.
3) Side margin is not required for over Bridges, cross over bridges,
   flyovers or subways.
   (However if there is enough space, then side margin can be kept).

Sanjay Harising Pardeshi
Sketch no. 100/117

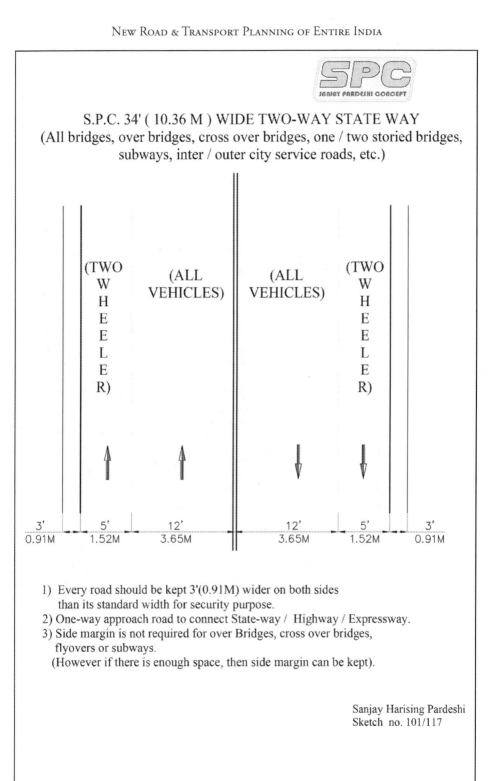

S.P.C. 34' (10.36 M) WIDE TWO-WAY STATE WAY
(All bridges, over bridges, cross over bridges, one / two storied bridges,
subways, inter / outer city service roads, etc.)

1) Every road should be kept 3'(0.91M) wider on both sides
   than its standard width for security purpose.
2) One-way approach road to connect State-way / Highway / Expressway.
3) Side margin is not required for over Bridges, cross over bridges,
   flyovers or subways.
   (However if there is enough space, then side margin can be kept).

Sanjay Harising Pardeshi
Sketch no. 101/117

Sanjay Harising Pardeshi
Sketch no. 102/117

S.P.C. 60' (18.29 M) WIDE TWO-WAY STATE WAY

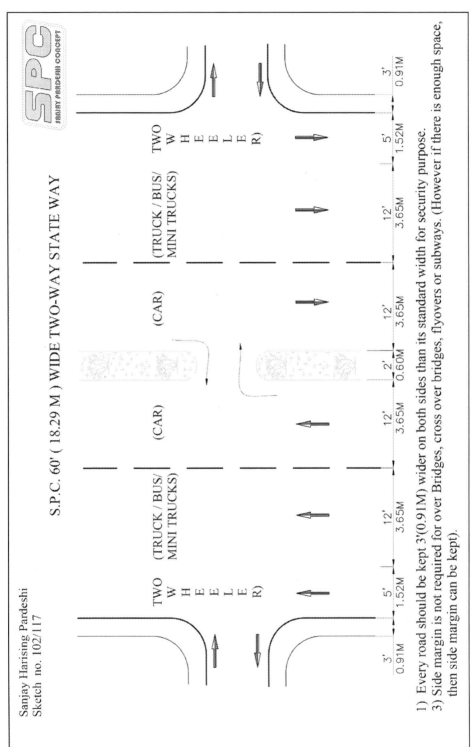

1) Every road should be kept 3'(0.91M) wider on both sides than its standard width for security purpose.
3) Side margin is not required for over Bridges, cross over bridges, flyovers or subways. (However if there is enough space, then side margin can be kept).

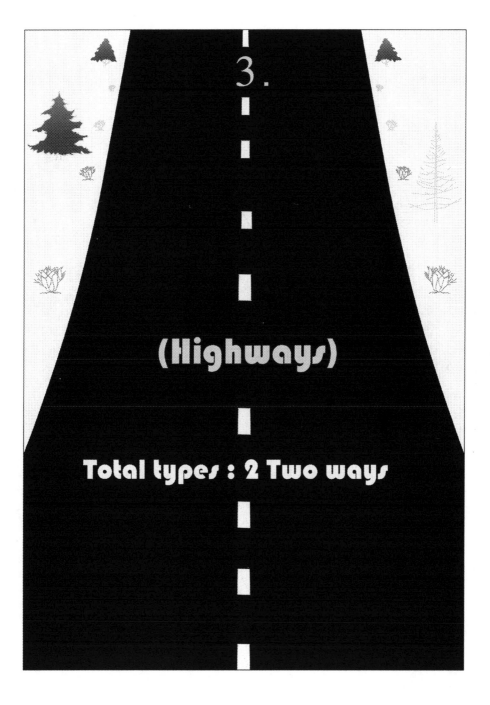

3.

(Highways)

Total types : 2 Two ways

Sanjay Harising Pardeshi
Sketch no. 103/117

S.P.C. 70' (21.34 M) WIDE TWO-WAY HIGHWAY

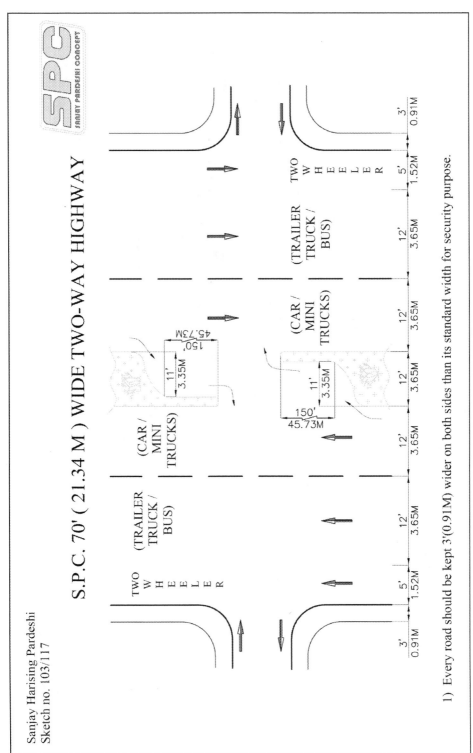

1) Every road should be kept 3'(0.91M) wider on both sides than its standard width for security purpose.

S.P.C. 90' (27.44 M) WIDE TWO-WAY HIGHWAY

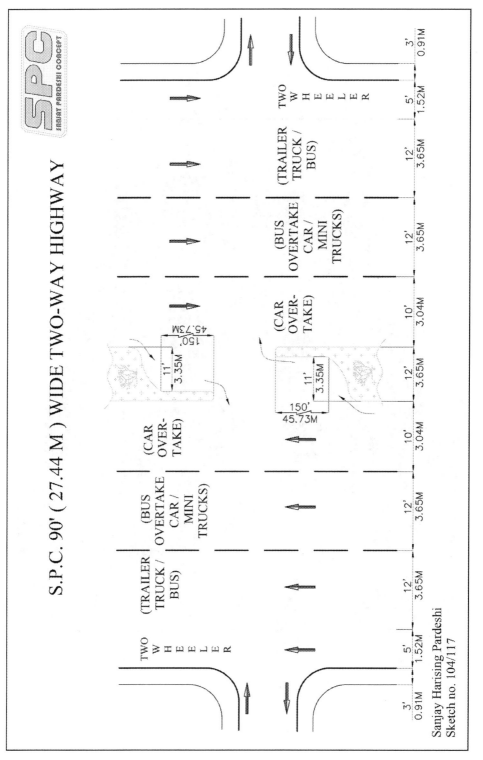

Sanjay Harising Pardeshi
Sketch no. 104/117

4.

(Expressways)

Total types : 8 two ways

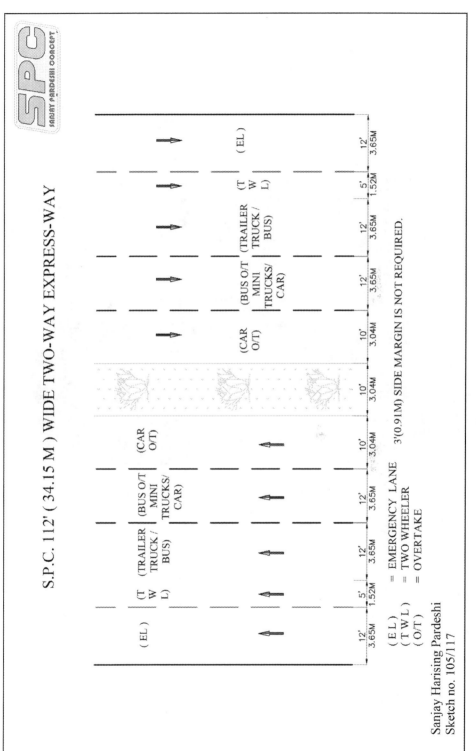

S.P.C. 112' (34.15 M) WIDE TWO-WAY EXPRESS-WAY

(E L) = EMERGENCY LANE
(T W L) = TWO WHEELER
(O/T) = OVERTAKE

3'(0.91M) SIDE MARGIN IS NOT REQUIRED.

Sanjay Harising Pardeshi
Sketch no. 105/117

Sanjay Harising Pardeshi
Sketch no. 106/117

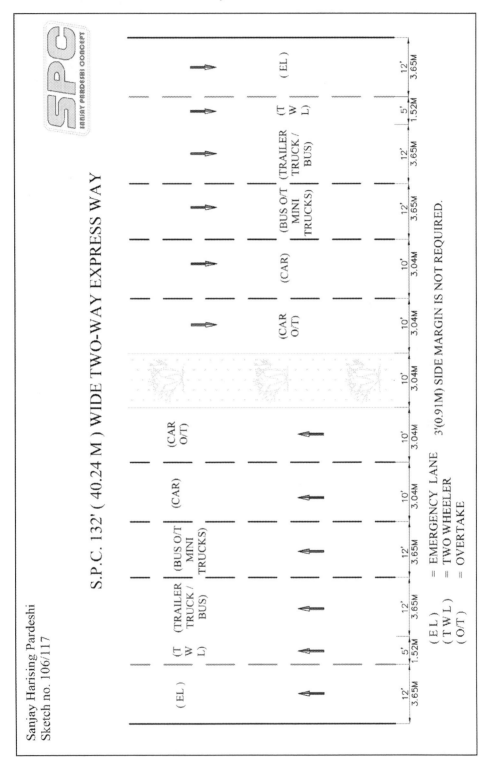

S.P.C. 132' (40.24 M) WIDE TWO-WAY EXPRESS WAY

(E L) = EMERGENCY LANE 3'(0.91M) SIDE MARGIN IS NOT REQUIRED.
(T W L) = TWO WHEELER
(O/T) = OVERTAKE

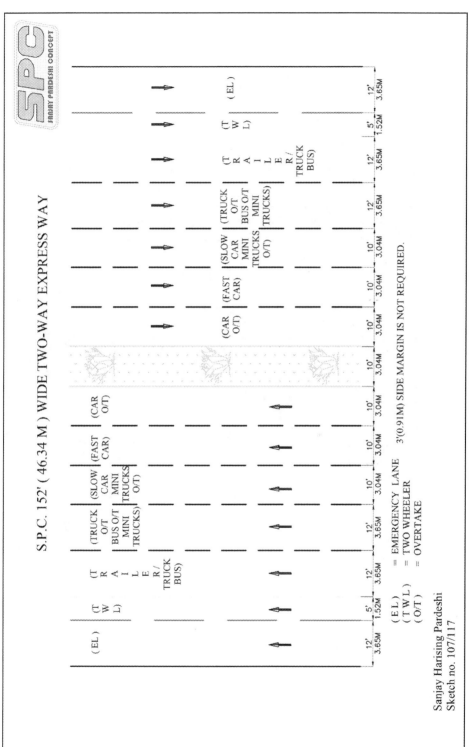

S.P.C. 152' (46.34 M) WIDE TWO-WAY EXPRESS WAY

Sanjay Harising Pardeshi
Sketch no. 107/117

(E L) = EMERGENCY LANE
(T W L) = TWO WHEELER
(O/T) = OVERTAKE

3'(0.91M) SIDE MARGIN IS NOT REQUIRED.

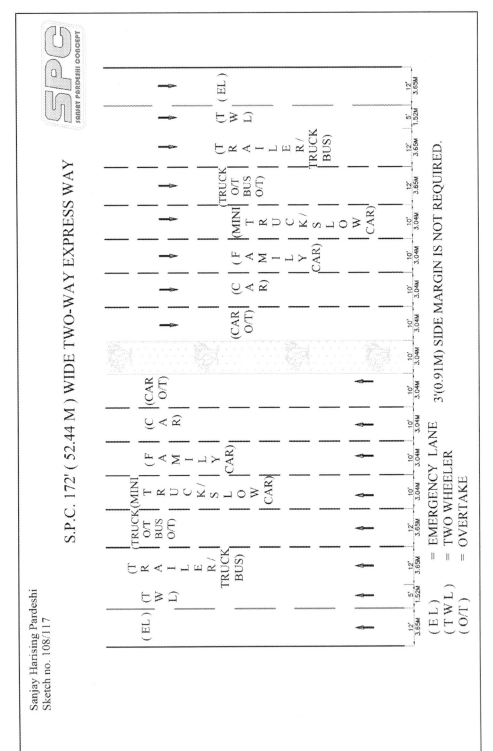

S.P.C. 172' (52.44 M) WIDE TWO-WAY EXPRESS WAY

Sanjay Harising Pardeshi
Sketch no. 108/117

(E L)   = EMERGENCY LANE
(T W L) = TWO WHEELER
(O/T)   = OVERTAKE

3'(0.91M) SIDE MARGIN IS NOT REQUIRED.

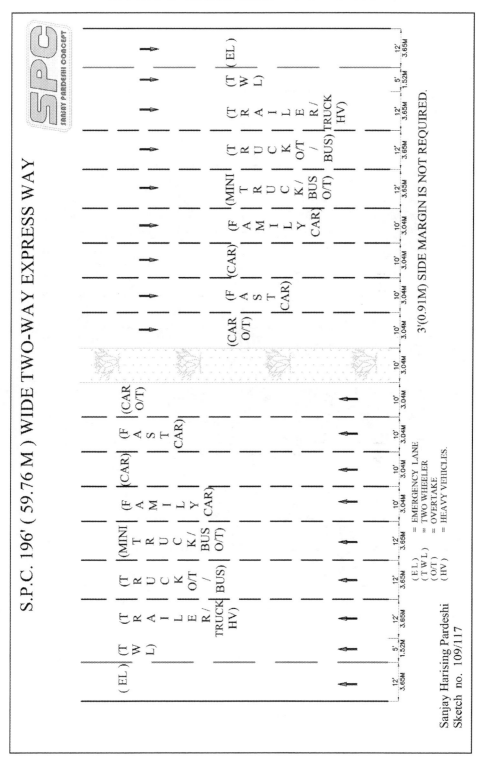

S.P.C. 196' (59.76 M) WIDE TWO-WAY EXPRESS WAY

Sanjay Harising Pardeshi
Sketch no. 109/117

(EL) = EMERGENCY LANE
(T W L) = TWO WHEELER
(O/T) = OVERTAKE
(HV) = HEAVY VEHICLES.

3'(0.91M) SIDE MARGIN IS NOT REQUIRED.

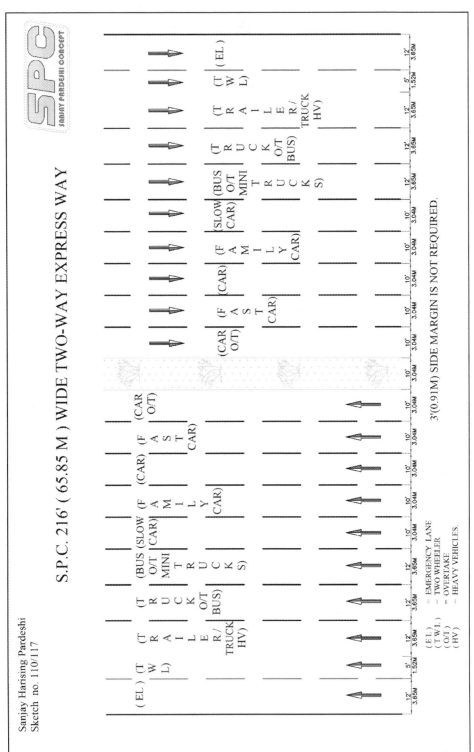

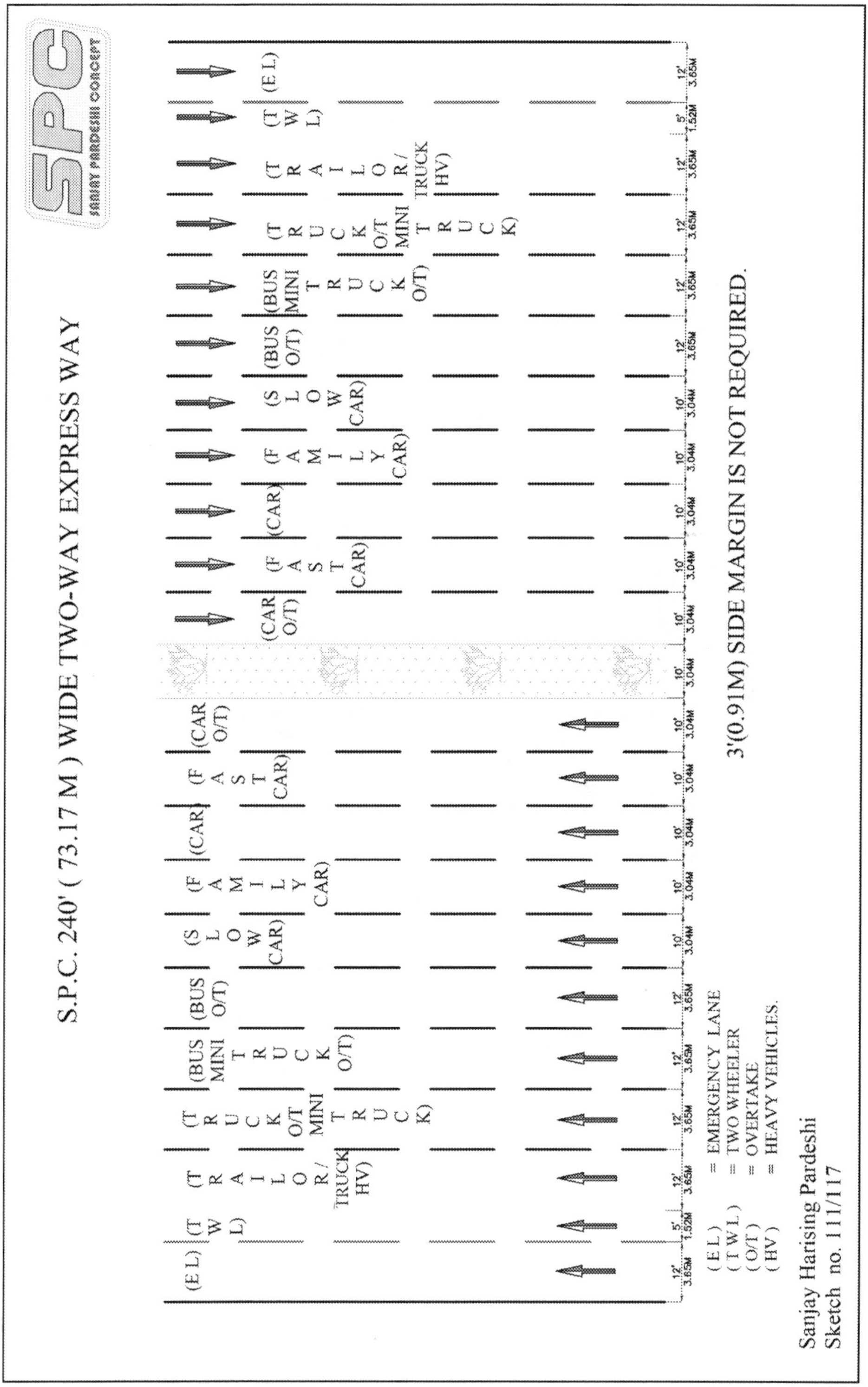

S.P.C. 240' (73.17 M) WIDE TWO-WAY EXPRESS WAY

SPC
SANJAY PARDESHI CONCEPT

3'(0.91M) SIDE MARGIN IS NOT REQUIRED.

(E L) = EMERGENCY LANE
(T W L) = TWO WHEELER
(O/T) = OVERTAKE
(HV) = HEAVY VEHICLES.

Sanjay Harising Pardeshi
Sketch no. 111/117

165

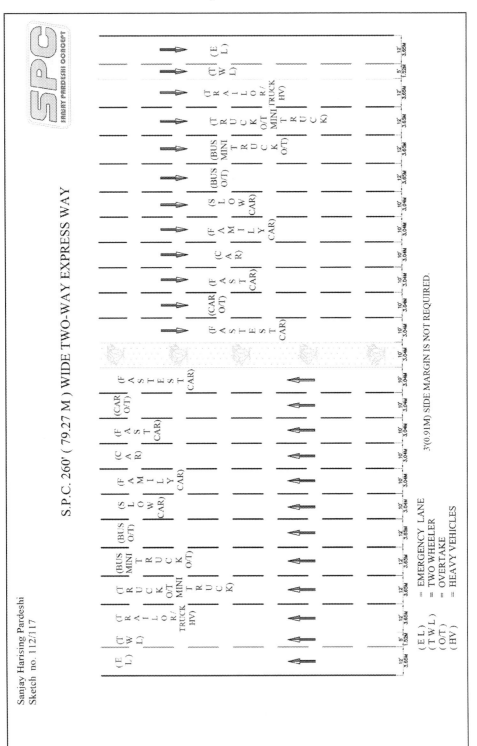

S.P.C. 260' (79.27 M) WIDE TWO-WAY EXPRESS WAY

Sanjay Harising Pardeshi
Sketch no. 112/117

(E L) = EMERGENCY LANE
(T W L) = TWO WHEELER
(O/T) = OVERTAKE
(HV) = HEAVY VEHICLES

3'(0.91M) SIDE MARGIN IS NOT REQUIRED.

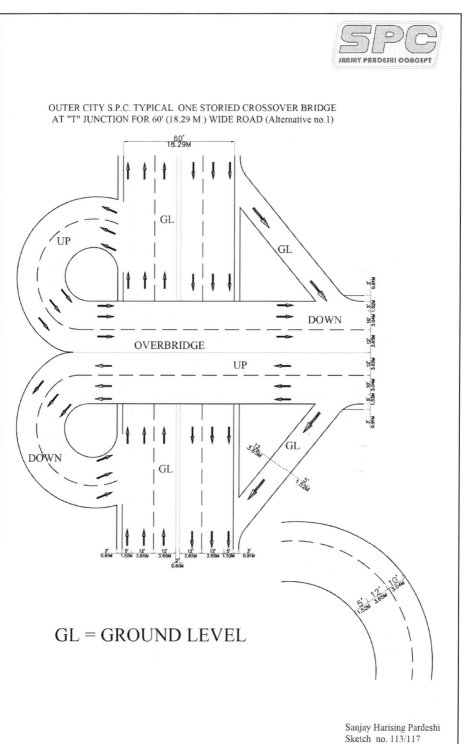

OUTER CITY S.P.C. TYPICAL ONE STORIED CROSSOVER BRIDGE
AT "T" JUNCTION FOR 60' (18.29 M) WIDE ROAD (Alternative no.1)

GL = GROUND LEVEL

Sanjay Harising Pardeshi
Sketch no. 113/117

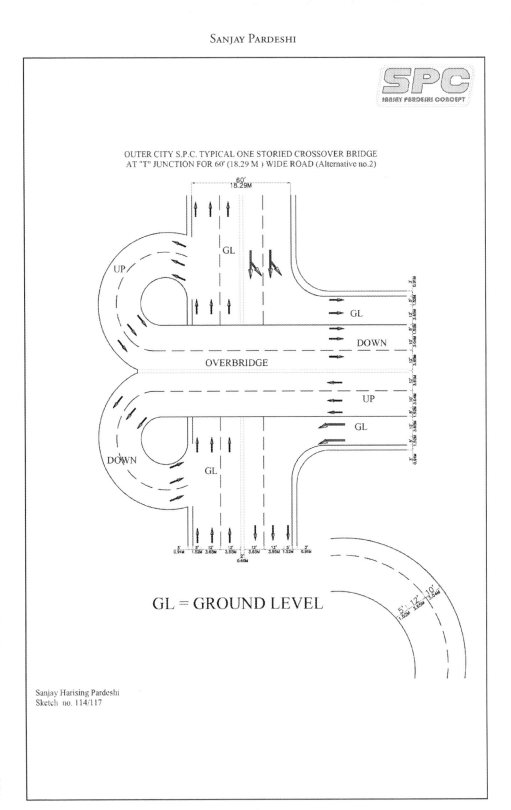

GL = GROUND LEVEL

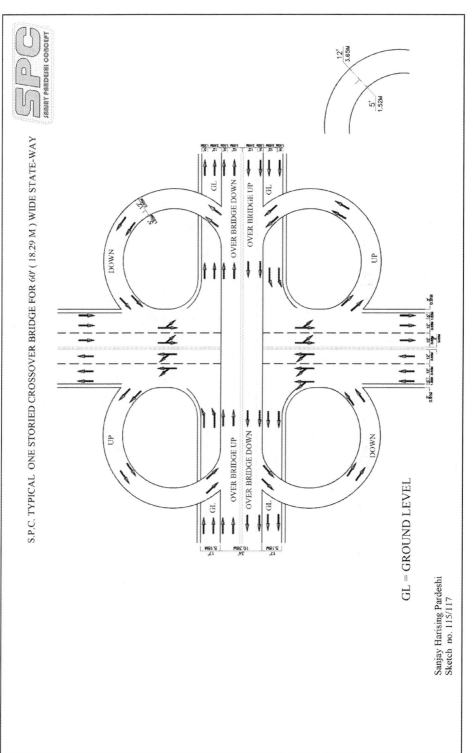

S.P.C. TYPICAL ONE STORIED CROSSOVER BRIDGE FOR 60' (18.29 M) WIDE STATE-WAY

GL = GROUND LEVEL

Sanjay Harising Pardeshi
Sketch no. 115/117

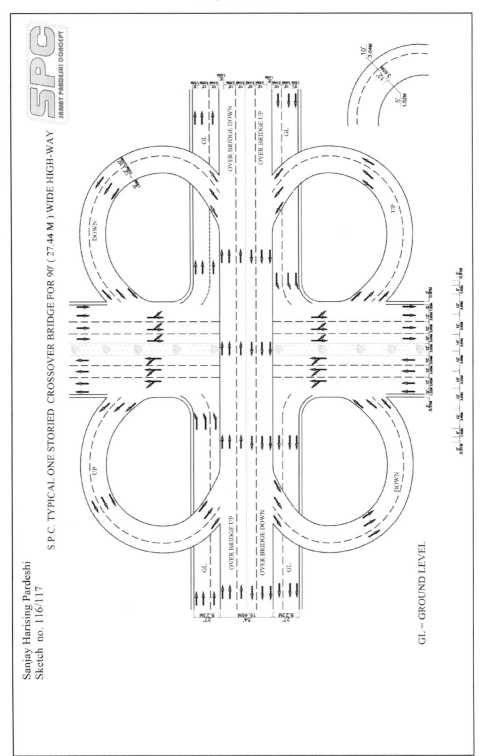

S.P.C. TYPICAL ONE STORIED CROSSOVER BRIDGE FOR 90' (27.44 M) WIDE HIGH-WAY

Sanjay Harising Pardeshi
Sketch no. 116/117

GL = GROUND LEVEL

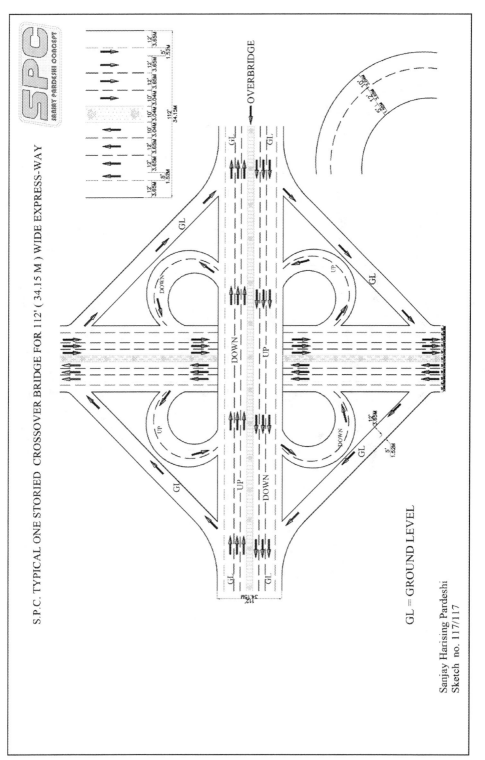

S.P.C. TYPICAL ONE STORIED CROSSOVER BRIDGE FOR 112' (34.15 M) WIDE EXPRESS-WAY

GL = GROUND LEVEL

Sanjay Harising Pardeshi
Sketch no. 117/117

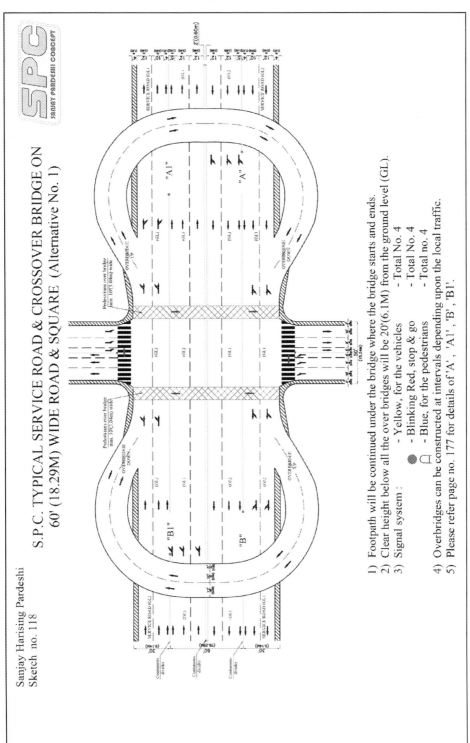

Sanjay Harising Pardeshi
Sketch no. 118

S.P.C. TYPICAL SERVICE ROAD & CROSSOVER BRIDGE ON
60' (18.29M) WIDE ROAD & SQUARE (Alternative No. 1)

1) Footpath will be continued under the bridge where the bridge starts and ends.
2) Clear height below all the over bridges will be 20'(6.1M) from the ground level (GL).
3) Signal system :
   - Yellow, for the vehicles   - Total No. 4
   - Blinking Red, stop & go   - Total No. 4
   - Blue, for the pedestrians   - Total no. 4
4) Overbridges can be constructed at intervals depending upon the local traffic.
5) Please refer page no. 177 for details of 'A' , 'A1' , 'B' , 'B1'.

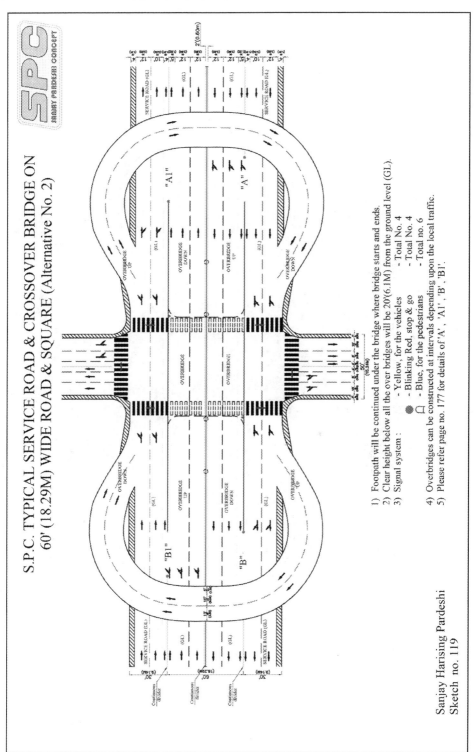

S.P.C. TYPICAL SERVICE ROAD & CROSSOVER BRIDGE ON
60' (18.29M) WIDE ROAD & SQUARE (Alternative No. 2)

1) Footpath will be continued under the bridge where bridge starts and ends.
2) Clear height below all the over bridges will be 20'(6.1M) from the ground level (GL).
3) Signal system :
   — Yellow, for the vehicles — Total No. 4
   — Blinking Red, stop & go — Total No. 4
   — Blue, for the pedestrians — Total no. 6
4) Overbridges can be constructed at intervals depending upon the local traffic.
5) Please refer page no. 177 for details of 'A', 'A1', 'B', 'B1'.

Sanjay Harising Pardeshi
Sketch no. 119

Sanjay Harising Pardeshi
Sketch no. 120

S.P.C. TYPICAL CONTINUOUS SERVICE ROAD & CROSSOVER BRIDGE ON 60' (18.29M) WIDE ROAD

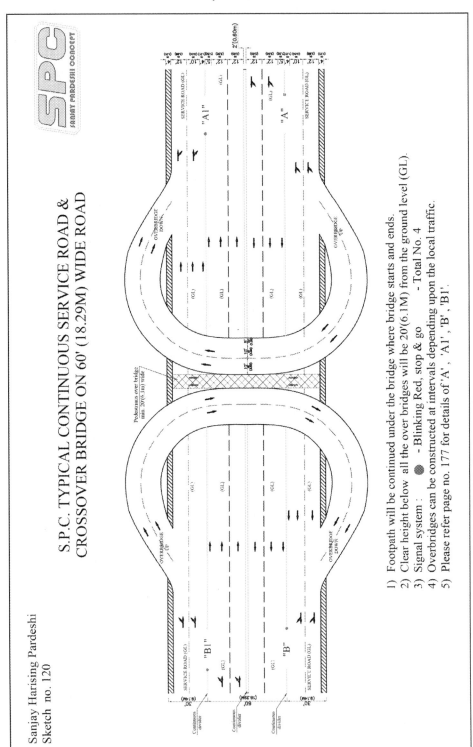

1) Footpath will be continued under the bridge where bridge starts and ends.
2) Clear height below all the over bridges will be 20'(6.1M) from the ground level (GL).
3) Signal system : ● - Blinking Red, stop & go   - Total No. 4
4) Overbridges can be constructed at intervals depending upon the local traffic.
5) Please refer page no. 177 for details of 'A', 'A1', 'B', 'B1'.

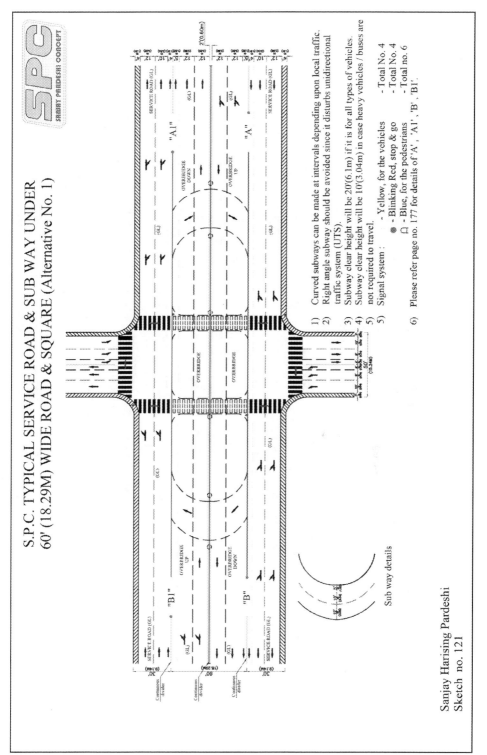

S.P.C. TYPICAL SERVICE ROAD & SUB WAY UNDER
60' (18.29M) WIDE ROAD & SQUARE (Alternative No. 1)

1) Curved subways can be made at intervals depending upon local traffic.
2) Right angle subway should be avoided since it disturbs unidirectional traffic system (UTS).
3) Subway clear height will be 20'(6.1m) if it is for all types of vehicles.
4) Subway clear height will be 10'(3.04m) in case heavy vehicles / buses are not required to travel.
5) Signal system :
   - Yellow, for the vehicles   - Total No. 4
   - Blinking Red, stop & go   - Total No. 4
   - Blue, for the pedestrians   - Total no. 6
6) Please refer page no. 177 for details of 'A', 'A1', 'B', 'B1'.

Sanjay Harising Pardeshi
Sketch no. 121

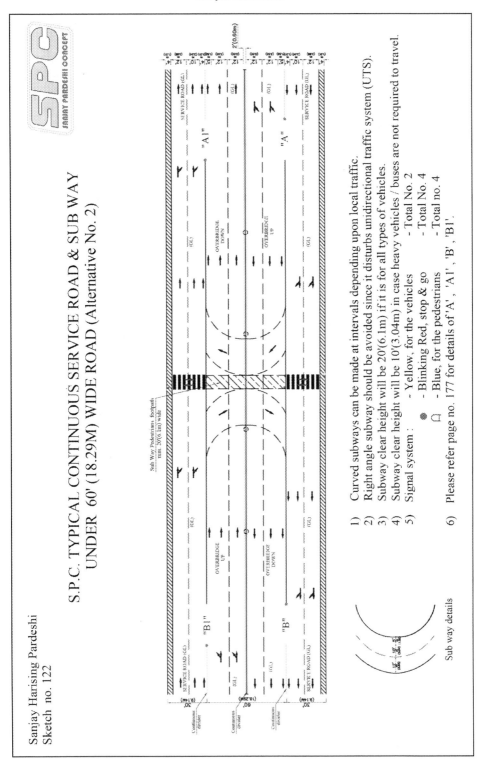

S.P.C. TYPICAL CONTINUOUS SERVICE ROAD & SUB WAY
UNDER 60' (18.29M) WIDE ROAD (Alternative No. 2)

1) Curved subways can be made at intervals depending upon local traffic.
2) Right angle subway should be avoided since it disturbs unidirectional traffic system (UTS).
3) Subway clear height will be 20'(6.1m) if it is for all types of vehicles.
4) Subway clear height will be 10'(3.04m) in case heavy vehicles / buses are not required to travel.
5) Signal system :   - Yellow, for the vehicles   - Total No. 2
                     - Blinking Red, stop & go   - Total No. 4
                     - Blue, for the pedestrians   - Total no. 4
6) Please refer page no. 177 for details of 'A', 'A1', 'B', 'B1'.

Sub way details

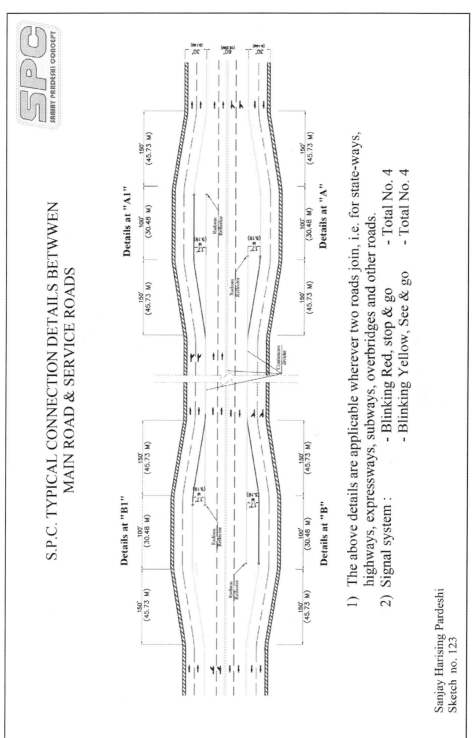

S.P.C. TYPICAL CONNECTION DETAILS BETWEEN MAIN ROAD & SERVICE ROADS

Details at "A1"

Details at "A"

Details at "B1"

Details at "B"

1) The above details are applicable wherever two roads join, i.e. for state-ways, highways, expressways, subways, overbridges and other roads.

2) Signal system :
    - Blinking Red, stop & go   - Total No. 4
    - Blinking Yellow, See & go   - Total No. 4

Sanjay Harising Pardeshi
Sketch no. 123

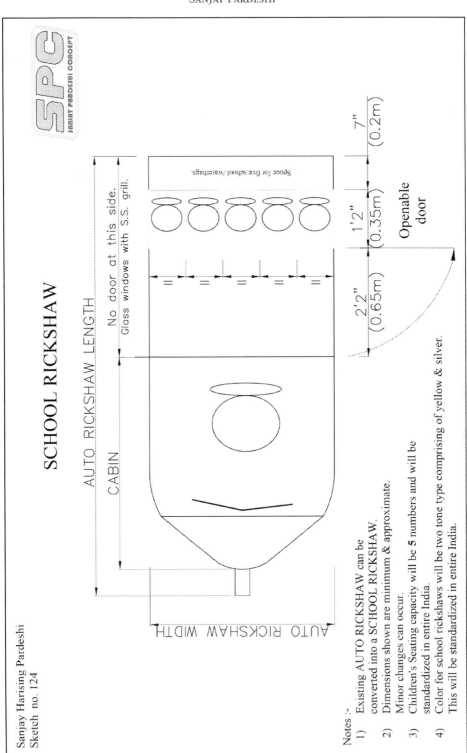

SCHOOL RICKSHAW

AUTO RICKSHAW LENGTH

CABIN

AUTO RICKSHAW WIDTH

No door at this side.
Glass windows with S.S. grill.

Space for five school waterbags.

2'2" (0.65m)

1'2" (0.35m)

7" (0.2m)

Openable door

Sanjay Harising Pardeshi
Sketch no. 124

Notes :-

1) Existing AUTO RICKSHAW can be converted into a SCHOOL RICKSHAW.

2) Dimensions shown are minimum & approximate. Minor changes can occur.

3) Children's Seating capacity will be **5** numbers and will be standardized in entire India.

4) Color for school rickshaws will be two tone type comprising of yellow & silver. This will be standardized in entire India.

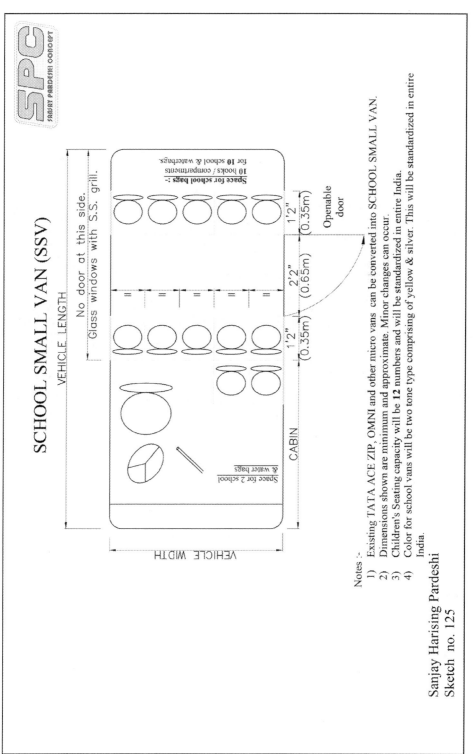

SCHOOL SMALL VAN (SSV)

VEHICLE LENGTH

No door at this side.
Glass windows with S.S. grill.

Space for school bags :-
10 hooks / compartments
for 10 school & waterbags.

VEHICLE WIDTH

CABIN

Space for 2 school
& water bags

1'2" (0.35m)

2'2" (0.65m)

1'2" (0.35m)

Openable door

Notes :-

1) Existing TATA ACE ZIP, OMNI and other micro vans can be converted into SCHOOL SMALL VAN.
2) Dimensions shown are minimum and approximate. Minor changes can occur.
3) Children's Seating capacity will be 12 numbers and will be standardized in entire India.
4) Color for school vans will be two tone type comprising of yellow & silver. This will be standardized in entire India.

Sanjay Harising Pardeshi
Sketch no. 125

Sanjay Harising Pardeshi
Sketch no. 126

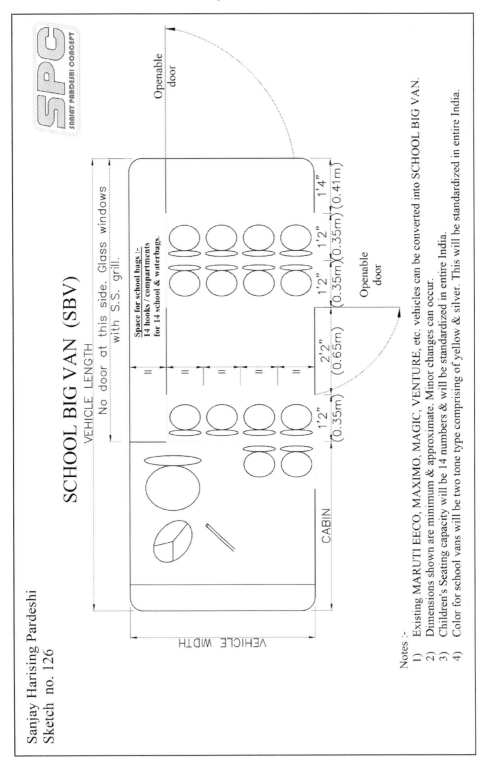

SCHOOL BIG VAN (SBV)

Notes :-

1) Existing MARUTI EECO, MAXIMO, MAGIC, VENTURE. etc. vehicles can be converted into SCHOOL BIG VAN.
2) Dimensions shown are minimum & approximate. Minor changes can occur.
3) Children's Seating capacity will be 14 numbers & will be standardized in entire India.
4) Color for school vans will be two tone type comprising of yellow & silver. This will be standardized in entire India.

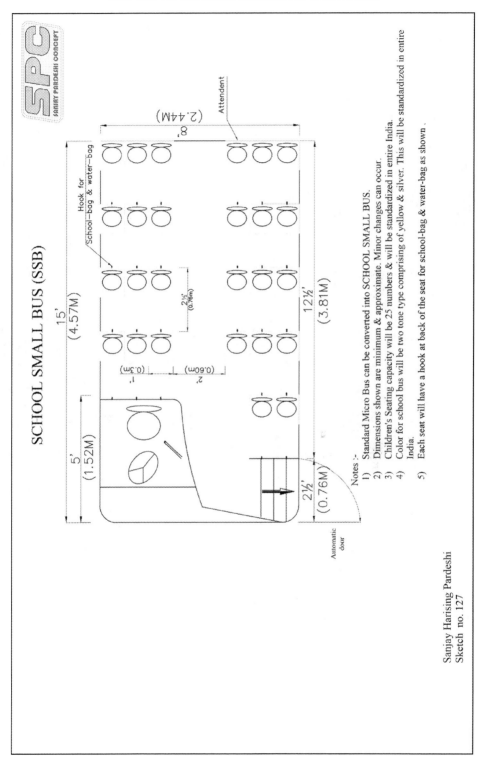

SCHOOL SMALL BUS (SSB)

Notes :-

1) Standard Micro Bus can be converted into SCHOOL SMALL BUS.
2) Dimensions shown are minimum & approximate. Minor changes can occur.
3) Children's Seating capacity will be 25 numbers & will be standardized in entire India.
4) Color for school bus will be two tone type comprising of yellow & silver. This will be standardized in entire India.
5) Each seat will have a hook at back of the seat for school-bag & water-bag as shown .

Sanjay Harising Pardeshi
Sketch no. 127

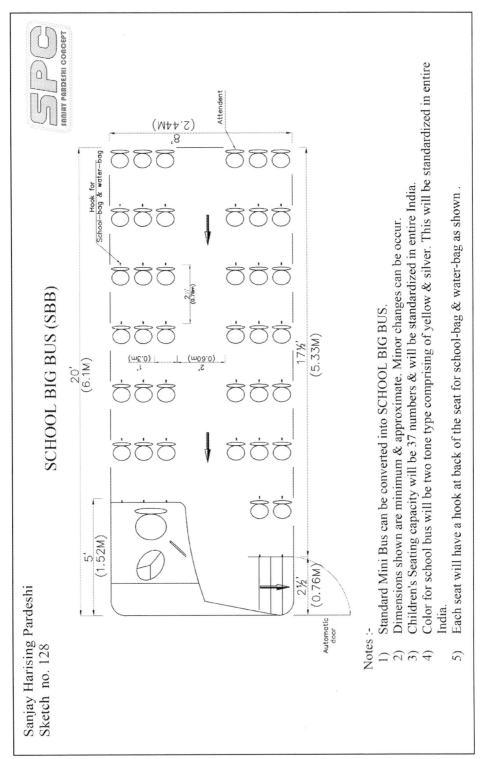

Sanjay Harising Pardeshi
Sketch no. 128

SCHOOL BIG BUS (SBB)

Notes :-

1) Standard Mini Bus can be converted into SCHOOL BIG BUS.

2) Dimensions shown are minimum & approximate. Minor changes can be occur.

3) Children's Seating capacity will be 37 numbers & will be standardized in entire India.

4) Color for school bus will be two tone type comprising of yellow & silver. This will be standardized in entire India.

5) Each seat will have a hook at back of the seat for school-bag & water-bag as shown.

S.P.C. ONE WAY BUS RAPID TRANSIT (BRT)
ON 60' (18.29 MTRS) WIDE ONE WAY CITY ROAD

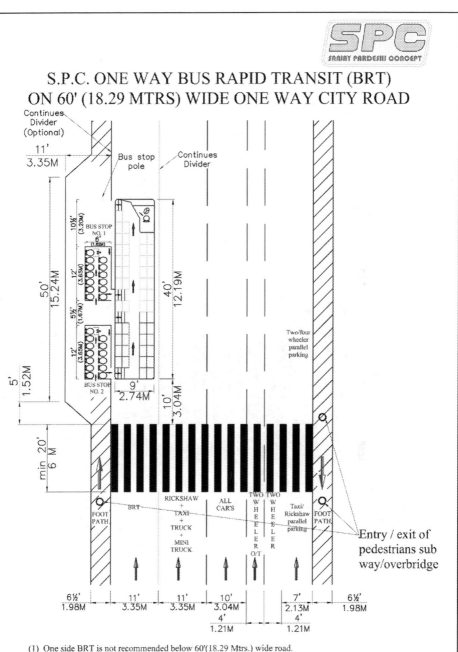

(1) One side BRT is not recommended below 60'(18.29 Mtrs.) wide road.
(2) Any other vehicles are not allowed in BRT lane.
(3) Refer Page No.146 for continuous dividers.
(4) Dividers will be installed continuously along with the BRT lane except zebra crossings.
(5) Zebra crossings will be at every 0.5 to 0.6 kms. and at the bus stop as shown on page No.123 to 127.
(6) Follow parking markings as per the page no. 91, 92, 93 & 94.
(7) If pedestrians over bridge or subway is to be built, then zebra crossing is not required and in that case divider will be continuous.

Sanjay Harising Pardeshi
Sketch no. 129

S.P.C. TWO WAY BUS RAPID TRANSIT (BRT)
ON 70' (21.34MTRS) WIDE ONE WAY CITY ROAD

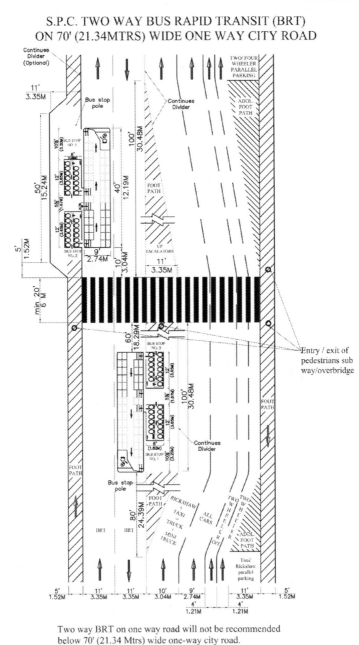

Two way BRT on one way road will not be recommended
below 70' (21.34 Mtrs) wide one-way city road.

Sanjay Harising Pardeshi
Sketch no. 130

S.P.C. TWO WAY BUS RAPID TRANSIT (BRT) ON 80' (24.39MTRS) WIDE ONE WAY CITY ROAD

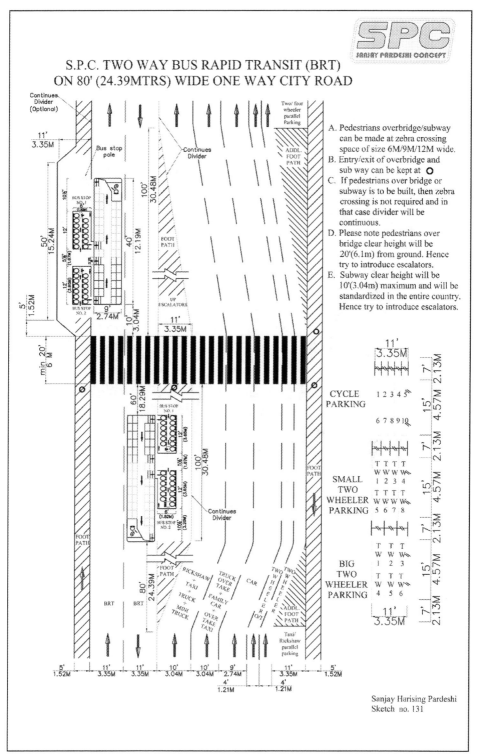

A. Pedestrians overbridge/subway can be made at zebra crossing space of size 6M/9M/12M wide.

B. Entry/exit of overbridge and sub way can be kept at O

C. If pedestrians over bridge or subway is to be built, then zebra crossing is not required and in that case divider will be continuous.

D. Please note pedestrians over bridge clear height will be 20'(6.1m) from ground. Hence try to introduce escalators.

E. Subway clear height will be 10'(3.04m) maximum and will be standardized in the entire country. Hence try to introduce escalators.

Sanjay Harising Pardeshi
Sketch no. 131

185

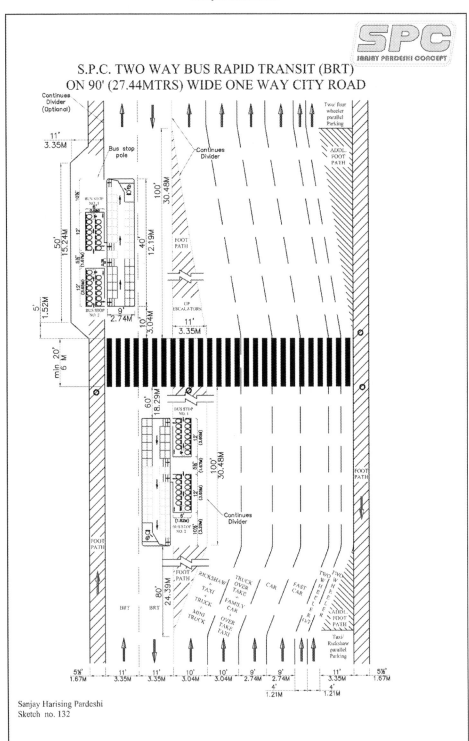

S.P.C. TWO WAY BUS RAPID TRANSIT (BRT)
ON 90' (27.44MTRS) WIDE ONE WAY CITY ROAD

Sanjay Harising Pardeshi
Sketch no. 132

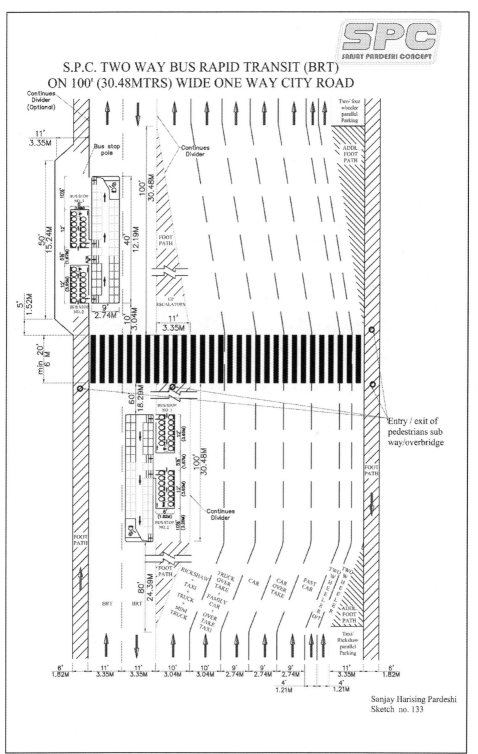

S.P.C. TWO WAY BUS RAPID TRANSIT (BRT)
ON 100' (30.48MTRS) WIDE ONE WAY CITY ROAD

Sanjay Harising Pardeshi
Sketch no. 133

S.P.C. TWO WAY BUS RAPID TRANSIT (BRT)
ON 120' (36.58 MTRS) WIDE TWO WAY CITY ROAD

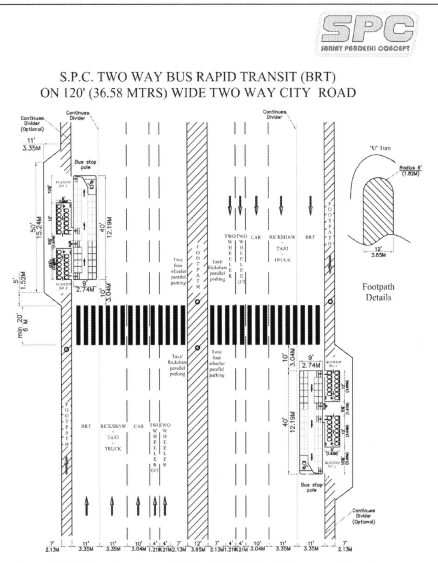

Footpath
Details

(1) BRT at both side will not be recommended below 120'(36.58 Mtrs.) wide two-way city road.
(2) Any other vehicles are not allowed in BRT lane.
(3) Refer Page No.146 for continuous dividers.
(4) Dividers will be installed continuously along with the BRT lane except zebra crossings.
(5) Zebra crossings will be at every 0.5 to 0.6 kms. and at the bus stop as shown.
(6) Follow parking markings as per the page no. 91, 92, 93 & 94.
(7) If pedestrians over bridge or subway is to be built, then zebra crossing is not required and in that case divider will be continuous.
(8) 'U' turn will be at every 0.5 to 0.6 km distance between the two bus stops (if required) and wherever needed.

Sanjay Harising Pardeshi
Sketch no. 134

Advantages of SPC Bus Rapid Transit (BRT) System over existing BRT system.

Existing BRT	SPC BRT
a. Runs in the middle of the road, hence disturbs complete road structure and needs major changes resulting in huge expenses.	**a.** Runs at left side of the road and hence does not disturb road structure, does not require any major changes resulting in minimum expenses refer page no. 183 to 188.
b. Different standardization/dimensions are required at different places to run on different roads.	**b.** Existing standard wider roads can be converted immediately (with minor changes) into BRT roads by just introducing continuous dividers along with BRT lane. e.g. existing 60'(18.29m) wide one-way or 120'(36.58m) wide two-way can be converted immediately since it has separate bus lanes already.
c. Needs new types of buses with right side doors, resulting in new investment.	c. Existing buses can be used. New investment is not required.
d. These new types of buses with right side doors requires left side doors also to run on existing routes apart from BRT, resulting in wastage of space in buses.	d. New types of left side four-door buses can be used for BRT as well as for existing routes in addition to existing buses resulting in space saving in all buses.
e. India has a right hand drive and left side traffic system, hence existing bus / bus stops / stands cannot be used. Needs to install all new bus stops / stands/dividers.	e. Existing bus stops / stands can be used. Needs additional bus stops only on those routes where two-way BRT is required on one-way road as per page no. 184 to 187.
f. Requires more space in the middle of the road to install two-way bus stops & two-way pedestrians subways / over bridges.	f. Requires half space in the middle of the road to install one-way bus stops & one-way pedestrians subways / over bridges.

Categories of the roads

SPC
SANJAY PARDESHI CONCEPT

Roads in Villages & Hilly Areas	Roads in Cities	Roads on Outskirts of Big Cities	State-ways	National Highways / Expressways
1) 12'(3.65m) w & 17'(5.18m) w (one-way), 24'(7.32m) w & 34'(10.36m) w (two-way). 2) Follow the city roads as per the requirement. 3) Follow standardization of state-way or city roads for the service roads.	1) 15'(4.57m) w to 100'(30.48m) w one-way & two-Way. 2) 120'(36.58m) w to 200'(60.98m) w two-way. Build service roads on both sides of standard roads wherever possible. 3) Follow standard city one/two/three storied overbridges for 'T' junctions/ square. 4) For roads more than 200'(60.98m) w roads, follow the expressways with service roads.	1) 112'(34.15m) w to 260'(79.27m)w expressway with service roads. 2) 120'(36.58m) w to 200'(60.98m)w two-way city roads with service roads. 3) If wider roads require more than 200'(60.98m) w two-way or 260'(79.27m)w expressway, increase number of standard lanes and build wider roads. This can be applicable inside and outside the cities also.	1) 12'(3.65m) w/ 17'(5.18m) w/ 27'(8.23m) w/ (one-way), 24'(7.32m) w/ 34'(10.36m) w/ 60'(18.29m) w (two-way), with service roads. 2) Follow standard over bridges and subway for crossing the roads.	1) State-way 60'(18.29m), Highway 70'(21.34m), Highway 90'(27.44m) & Expressway 112'(34.15m), these four types of roads will cover maximum transportation of entire country. Hence maximum construction of these roads is necessary. 2) If required, follow more wide standard express ways. 3) Follow standard over bridges and subways for crossing the roads. **Total Types of Roads = 45 Nos.**

Categories of the Transportation System

A. Public Transportation System

● **Standard Buses**

1. Big Double Decker	: Seat Capacity 86
2. Small Double Decker	: Seat Capacity 64
3. Big Bus	: Seat Capacity 49
4. Bus	: Seat Capacity 39
5. Small Bus	: Seat Capacity 31
6. Mini Bus	: Seat Capacity 23
7. Micro Bus	: Seat Capacity 15

● **Standard Taxies**

1. Share Big Taxi	: Seat Capacity 12
2. Share Small Taxi	: Seat Capacity 8
3. Private Big Taxi	: Seat Capacity 5
4. Private Small Taxi	: Seat Capacity 5

B. Luggage Transportation System (Goods Carrier)

1. Standard Light Commercial Vehicles (LCV)	: Total type 4
2. Standard Trucks	: Total type 4
3. Standards Trailers	: Total type 4

C. Other Standardizations

● **Standard Bus Stops**

1. Single Row	: Seat Capacity 7
2. Double Row	: Seat Capacity 13
3. Four Row	: Seat Capacity 25

Total Types of Vehicles :
7 Buses + 4 Taxies + 12 goods carrier = 23
(Excluding Private Cars & Two-wheelers)

JAI HIND !!!

Seven tunes of 'How To Revive India'

1) 'BHARAT BADALE' : Indian people doing the biggest work for their newly developing nation after independence.

2) India's completely new BASIC REVOLUTIONARY PLANS (BRPs) & INFRASTRUCTURE DEVELOPMENT PLANS (IDPs) for 'BHARAT BADALE'.

3) 300 days work yearly - India will develop rapidly.

4) Economy, agriculture, education, health, justice & Government Administration . . . BRP Department's direct solutions.

5) Water, electricity, residence, drainage / garbage, roads & transportation . . . IDP Department's basic solutions.

6) Control the population ! All happy in the nation !!

7) HAMARA BHARAT, HUM SAB MILKAR BADALE !!

SANJAY PARDESHI CONCEPT (SPC)